THE LAST
MOUNTAIN

THE LAST MOUNTAIN

LINCOLN E. STEED

Pacific Press Publishing Association
Boise, Idaho
Oshawa, Ontario, Canada

This is a true story. To protect people still living, some names have been changed, and small changes have been made to the dialogue.

Edited by Randy Maxwell
Designed by Tim Larson
Cover by Linda Griffith
Cover photo by Galen Rowell
Typeset in 10/12 Century Schoolbook

Library of Congress Catalog Card Number: 89-69856

ISBN 0-8163-0899-3

90 91 92 93 94 • 5 4 3 2 1

CONTENTS

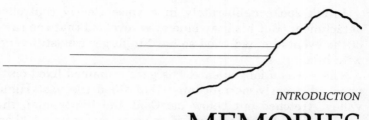

MEMORIES

*T*he day Snesia died. . . ."
     A passing cloud obscured the sun for a few moments, and the air chilled perceptibly. Frank Kelly reached deeper into the past he could not forget.

"It happened on Valentine's Day."

He paused at the irony of that statement.

"A wonderfully mild, sun-drenched February day in 1982. Snesia and her instructor—" He practically spat the word *instructor*. ". . . went climbing at Seneca Rocks in Virginia. She went without me because he said that I was dangerous—a threat to the safety of their expedition.

"The rocks were miserably cold. Too cold to climb safely. The sun was shining, but the rocks were in shadow and icy cold. . . .

"At first I blamed God. 'Why didn't You take me instead? Why didn't You give me the chance to die with her?'

"I would have instantly flung myself over that rock face after her—if I had been there. But she was alone.

"We had been so close. So close I felt I could almost hold her soul in my hands. Then it slipped through my fingers, and she was gone forever."

Frank spoke deliberately in a voice clearly controlled into detachment. But his gray-blue eyes revealed that the raw shock of the events he had tried so hard to forget was still very much with him.

There was a long silence. His gaze remained fixed on the impenetrable early-morning mist that filled the vast Himalayan valley stretched out below us. Cold and impersonal, the mist would recede like the waves of an ocean one moment, then come swirling back up the valley sides, spilling over the edge at our feet and enveloping us in cold darkness the next.

"So your wife's death was the catalyst for you to drop out of society?" I had to keep the interview going. The tape recorder was scraping away on the wicker table between us, regardless of mist or long pauses.

"Yes, after her death, I gave up any pretense of playing the success games. There are more important concerns than the conventions of modern society. I needed answers to so many things. For a long time I had felt that middle-class American life was cheating me—that I didn't belong.

"So when my wife died, I said goodbye to all of it. Everything. I became a wanderer—wandering the earth's surface in search of an answer.

"At first I thought the answer would come with finding another wife. But I soon realized it was deeper than that. The true answer lay in discovering my place in the overall scheme of things. The true answer lay in finding a way past the tragedy and confusion of my life.

"I found my answers here," said Frank with a wide sweep of his arm toward the nearby village and along the mountain ridge.

There was a settled certainty in his last statement. It had to be true. As I looked across at him, I saw a man at peace with himself. He looked far younger than his forty years. His hair was dark, and his eyes were alive and animated. Tall and athletically slim, Frank Kelly hardly looked like a man back from beyond the edge of hope. His almost unlined face told no open tale of troubles.

Yet looking closer, I saw a small patch of white on one cheek. It appeared cold and dead as though touched by a winter frost. It had been bitterly cold for the last five years!

"Snesia's death cut my ties to society," Frank continued. "I was actually dead myself—an empty husk. I was free to put my pack on my back and leave the world I no longer wanted. It was a long journey. It's over now."

The mist was rapidly pulling back from our vantage point above the valley. It was now rolling downwards, while at the same time becoming transparent in the encroaching sunlight.

And suddenly there they were—the peaks of the Himalayas—Everest, Annapurna, and dozens of other practically unassailable mountains, crowding the horizon in dazzling white.

"I came looking for mountains and found much more," Frank said simply.

"Let's go back to the beginning," I prompted, half afraid we would miss the true continuity of the story by explaining its conclusion.

"You've got it." Frank smiled. "Just load up that tape player and let's go. There's plenty to tell."

AND SO BEGINS the true story of an incredible journey and an incredible search. The journey stretches across continents and years. It is a story of great pain, great adventure, and, ultimately, great fulfillment.

There above the stair-step gardens clinging to green Himalayan foothills, Dr. Frank Kelly relived the past—a past that became the present again as we, through tape-recorded interviews and hand-scribbled notes, entered into his great adventure.

Nearby, an accordionlike instrument played the same hauntingly oriental song over and over again. It gradually faded as the story progressed. Even the sound of the gently scraping tape recorder receded from the emerging past.

1
BREAKING AWAY

*F*rank Kelly leaned into the white-cold wind that sliced great gashes in the undulating snowdrifts, and pushed his way along the track leading out of Ely, Minnesota. It was late in the evening, a time normally reserved for darkness and quiet. Tonight it was white and noisy. And yet, Frank felt more alone than he had for days.

He had spent the entire day reading in the university library. It was quiet in the library and easier to hear the books talking. For months, books had been his traveling companions and confidants out on the lakes and rivers. Now the waters had frozen, and books were for warm places.

At first, the librarians thought his rough, unkempt appearance a sign of ignorance. They knew better now and treated him as a regular—one of the library family. They now expected the beard, long hair, secondhand felt-lined boots, and a worn jacket.

When questioned as to why he spent so much time in the library, Frank answered simply, "I like to read." It was true, in a way. He did like to read. But he read all day to forget. Sometimes he thought he would never forget.

Ahead of him the track ended abruptly. He stopped, knowing by memory what lay ahead, gasping cautiously for the air warmed in the face tunnel of his parka. It was the ice cliff at last. Cautiously, Frank slipped his feet into the familiar notches and worked his way down the short but steep drop-off. It was his special satisfaction that his way down was a secret one and that no one could follow.

At the bottom of the cliff the ground flattened and stretched out to meet the white wind. The "ground" was actually the frozen surface of a lake. Here, on the lake, at the bottom of a cliff, was home.

Frank turned to one side of the bank and moved toward the rounded shape almost hidden in the white landscape. He was proud of the snow cave. It had only taken about six hours to build, and yet many weeks later it was intact and offering good low-cost shelter.

Few people, he mused, understood how practical a snow cave really was. Inside, it was light and cozy. It kept the wind and weather outside. Winter gales were muffled to insignificance through the tightly packed walls of snow, and even the cold was filtered by ice to something far closer to the freezing point.

As Frank waded through the snow to his ice-cave home, he was already mentally inside and checking over the familiar things. There was his pack—tested companion of many months outdoors. Rolled up next to it was the down sleeping bag that guaranteed protection from the lethal Minnesota winter. Next to it were the two blankets he had purchased for $4 each. They were extra insurance against extraordinarily cold nights. But so far, even at -40° F, he had not needed the second blanket. Then there was a stack of assorted outdoor gear: carefully handcrafted cross-country skis of his own design, snowshoes, and a hand-woven rope. Of course there were other incidentals like pots, pans, portable stove, and food. All familiar things filling his closed world of the ice cave.

The entrance was covered by drifting snow. Frank bent down and scooped it away before crawling through the slight tunnel of an entrance. Now he would have some relief from the cold. It was at least -10° F outside. He switched on his flashlight and swept the beam around the interior.

Empty! There was nothing inside the cave. Nothing! Someone had taken all his belongings. For a moment, Frank was so stunned he just stared in disbelief. Then in a frenzy he scrambled about the snow floor for his document pack—gone too. His passport and personal papers were gone. And the thief had taken the treasured pack of keepsakes he regularly took out whenever he thought of her. It was a last reminder—now gone, forever.

Outside, the wind whined disconsolately. It was going to be a miserably cold night. There was no sense in going back to town—too late to even begin to get help. Too late to track the thief—the snow had drifted over any and all tracks. He would have to spend the night here with only his outdoor clothes and parka as protection. It would be cold. But then, he was used to the cold.

Frank crouched up on the sleeping ledge in something approaching an upright fetal position and began the long wait for dawn. Nothing to do but wait. Plenty of time to think . . . to remember . . . back to when it all began . . . back across the years. . . .

* * * * *

"You will be throwing away all of the advantages we've given you!" The elder Frank Kelly was emphatic and angry. His voice, constricted by emotion, seemed even more distant and powerless over the phone. "What sort of a wild idea is this? Give me one good reason for wanting to quit your premed course!"

Frank thought of his father's office once more to remind himself of the main reason for his decision. "I'm just not sure that medicine is what I want, Dad. That's all."

But that wasn't all. Inside he was panic-stricken. He was panic-stricken at the vision of his future he'd been seeing lately. It was of a future very much like his father's.

His father was a respected and successful psychiatrist. That was the big plus as others saw it. A plus complete with a more-than-adequate income and job security. Frank's panic, however, was caused by another, less attractive side to medicine.

Frank saw his father going to work, day after day, year after year, to the same small office and the same four walls with the same pictures on them, listening to the same problems, from faces that changed only slightly from day to day.

"Were your grades falling, Frank? You've got to keep them

high to get into medical school."

"Hardly. Don't you remember, I was just recently invited to join the Loyola University honor society?"

"Well, yes, I do. But maybe you're not keeping your mind on your studies, just the same."

Keeping his mind on his studies! Too much so, in the estimation of most of his friends and classmates at the university. Two years ago he had graduated from McQuaid Jesuit High School near the top of his class, well prepared for the grind of a premed program. That didn't seem to prove anything, though, and Frank continued to be obsessive about studies and good grades.

In a way, the obsession with grades had been just another manifestation of the rule of the Kelly household. Excel in your primary education, excel at your secondary education, and go on to a professional school and become affluent as soon as possible.

It might have seemed rather self-centered but for the other elements constantly invoked by his parents and their church's institutions—honesty, straight dealings, pious service, and patriotism.

"I'm studying, Dad, and I've been doing well in my grades. But I've decided I want to take a different tack career-wise."

"Different!" His father coughed out the word. "You always wanted medicine. It's served me well and given you and your brothers and sisters a good life. We always expected you to take medicine and become a successful doctor. Think of the future, boy."

Yes, he had been thinking of the future a lot lately. Vietnam had put a pretty big cloud over a lot of that future. Maybe the world wouldn't make it past the sixties! Beyond apocalypse, though, the reoccurring image of a monotonous existence trapped in an office made the future seem cold and uninviting.

"Always expected." Well, maybe they had expected too much of him. Why did he have to do everything they wanted, anyway?

"I have made up my mind, Dad." He had decided to get to the point and brave the storm of objection. "I am transferring to the University of Michigan next year to take . . ." *brace yourself, Frank,* ". . . forestry and wildlife management."

"Well, at least you have a plan." The response was tight, controlled. Not the rage Frank had feared, but clearly not approval. "You've already put in two years at Loyola—toward medicine—how many more years to finish this forestry degree?"

Frank held the telephone receiver closer to his lips to make sure his father heard the reply. "Two, probably three more years."

"Hmmm, I guess you could waste your time less profitably. Maybe it will get this outdoor bug out of your system. Remember, medicine is more practical, son." It sounded like a parting shot to Frank, and he braced for the inevitable follow-up.

"Well, remember who's paying your bills. Stick to it, and whatever you do, give it your best. Oh, and one last thing. You finish that course before you think of any more crazy schemes, like getting married. I am insisting on that, Frank. No marriage till you graduate."

"Yes, it's a deal, Dad." Time to wind down what hadn't been all that bad a break with his father's plans. Now he could begin work on his own agenda.

"Bye."

"Bye."

Click. The receiver sounded off as Frank returned it to its cradle. And the two men were again far apart. His father back in their hometown of Rochester, New York, and Frank in Chicago, on the frontier of his new plans.

A feeling of freedom engulfed Frank as the reality of his decision to break away from the pull of his parent's aspirations began to sink in.

He knew that his mother, Mary Rose Kelly, would be disappointed. She had such high hopes for his medical career. But Frank had long ago realized that his mother's plans for him satisfied her own needs rather than his.

Mary Rose had met Frank's father at the hospital where they both worked. She was a nurse, idealistic and single. He was a doctor, recently widowed and needing companionship. Their courtship had been brief, followed quickly by marriage. And then came the fear that her husband was still in love with his first wife, who had died after only one year of marriage, shortly before Mary Rose had met him.

Frank's older stepbrother, Jerry, was the continual reminder of that first love. Mary Rose had come to resent him as the symbol of the love she could not understand. Frank was her eldest son, and she now needed him to regain from her husband what she felt was lost to Jerry. Frank could draw back her husband's first love. Of course, Frank had to be a doctor like his father!

Frank had known this tension for a long time. There had been no sudden revelation of his parent's real aspirations for him. His reaction had been building for years. Maybe it was just a moment of panic. But halfway through four years of college, the frightening vision of life imprisoned by the walls of a doctor's office seemed too real—too close. He had to get away from that nightmare. He had to be free—to live outdoors, where he had always wanted to be. A forestry degree would legitimize that need. It was the only choice he could have made.

2

THE SNOW
MAIDEN

*F*rank heard the happy music and laughter long before he
reached the gymnasium.

It had been a long week. His second year of forestry studies
was challenging, although he still had trouble reconciling what
he was learning with his concept of what a wildlife manager
needed to know. For tonight, however, he could forget studies,
forget exams, even forget any new operations for the Raider
Platoon—a Green Berets–type division of the University of
Michigan ROTC he had joined and become commander of.
Tonight was for relaxation.

Ahead of him at the end of the campus walkway, the concrete
rose in broad, beckoning steps to the open door of Waterman
Gym. It was dark and still along the pathway. The evening air
cast a foggy chill over the wet lawn that sprawled like carpeting
on either side. Frank needed the social interaction offered by the
Folk Dancing Club. His heart gave a few unexpected lurches as
he anticipated the prospect of light music and pleasant conversation.

Entering the gym, he stopped and looked around. There were
about eighty club members already there. A few had paired off

17

and were diligently practicing a new folk-dance routine. Most of the others were gathered in animated little groups, laughing and conversing happily.

"Now just remember," he told himself as he cast an eye over some of the young girls present, "nothing serious. You don't want to get involved."

But maybe he really did want to get involved. How else could he explain to himself a succession of impossible relationships that seemed promising at first but wound up imprisoning him with a sense of obligation. It seemed only right to make a commitment, but inevitably, that commitment bound him to a person he finally found plain and boring. What a dilemma. Better to play the field and play safe. Take your time, Frank.

Besides, he was casually dating several very pleasant girls. He wasn't looking for anybody in particular. He wasn't a hungry, predatory male. He just needed to socialize, to lighten up a little. And this was the place.

"Hello, Frank." It was a girl he had dated once or twice and found friendly, but shallow.

"Hello, Kathy," he answered in an offhand way, designed to keep her at a distance.

"Are you with anyone tonight, Frank?" She wouldn't let up.

"No—I just came over to check out the scene. See what's going on." There must be a way to shake her. He scanned the dancers for familiar faces, for new faces.

There—that girl—he hadn't seen her before. He watched her mastering the steps to a new dance. He watched her lithe movements, her unaffected enthusiasm. Her eyes sparkled with laughter. He had to meet her.

The dance ended, and he moved across the gym to intercept the girl with the laughing eyes as she left the dance floor. This would be relatively easy. He had made himself known to girls before like this. What's more, he had the advantage of being a fourth-year student, and she was obviously a freshman. She was bound to be impressed by his approach.

"Hello, there. My name's Frank—what's yours?" He spoke the line confidently and looked into her eyes for the answer.

"Snesiana Zdravkovich," she began, and for a moment, Frank heard nothing more. He was drawn into her eyes. What was happening? He noticed the curious lilt to her voice. It was captivating. Beyond that, he was instantly submerged in a strangely deepening awareness. This had never happened before.

Snesiana looked at him quizzically. "Do you come here often, Frank?" she asked, aware that he had momentarily lost the ability to carry a conversation.

He didn't hear the words clearly. He heard the vulnerability in her voice. He felt a need to reach out and protect her. "Every week," he answered in a daze, "but I've never seen you before."

She smiled like a little girl. "I'm new at the university. This is my first week. Some of the girls in the dorm said the dance club was a good place to meet people, so I came tonight to see what it was like."

"You have the most beautiful accent," commented Frank, still in a daze, but anxious to understand the captivating lilt to her voice.

"My family emigrated from Yugoslavia three years ago. I guess I still speak with a bit of an accent, Frank?"

"Nooo, not an accent—a special way of speaking." He wasn't making it up. He found her voice irresistible.

She smiled again in innocence, as though she somehow believed what would normally have been an improbable explanation.

"Your name . . . ?" He knew it was special, but only its sound lingered in his wildly racing mind.

"Snesiana," she said almost as a prompt.

"What does it mean?" Frank asked, somehow certain her name held deep meaning.

"My parents tell me it comes from a Russian word that means 'Snow White' or 'snow maiden.'" She watched her explanation sink in, eyes sparkling.

"Let's go where we can talk," suggested Frank impulsively. He had to learn more about this gangly, beautiful girl with the captivating manner.

Together they walked out of the crowded gymnasium and into the night. Just a little earlier, Frank had walked the same footpath and felt the press of darkness and cold—felt the need for the comfort of the crowd. Now everything was turned upside down. He was glad to be away from the clamor of the dance gathering. It was no longer lonely outside. This newfound creature at his side seemed to radiate light and warmth into his life.

"How do you like university life?" asked Frank as a way to continue the conversation.

Snesiana's eyes lighted up with boundless enthusiasm. "Oh, I just love it here. Already, in just the one week, I've met so many friends." Frank bristled inside at her obviously naive contacts. He would need to protect this little girl from the marauding hordes of male students—especially the upperclassmen like himself.

"It is so different from Yugoslavia, but already I feel at home," she continued.

"And where is your home now, Snesiana?" pursued Frank, with more than academic interest.

"Well, of course, I live in the campus dorm now. But home is still where my parents and younger brother live. It's not too far away—only fifteen miles from here in South Lyon, Michigan."

"My home is quite a long way from here," volunteered Frank automatically. "My parents live in Rochester, New York. But I don't feel too close to home anymore. I'm on my own now." He felt a stab of loneliness as he said it. He was hungry for human closeness—a need he had been ignoring.

The lights and noise from Waterman Gym were now muted by distance. Frank and Snesiana slowed to a more casual step and continued their conversation.

"What course are you taking, Snesiana?" Frank still spoke her name in such an awed tone that the young girl hardly knew what to make of it. "My family and friends call me Snesia," she suggested, hoping that would relax this interesting but overly formal fellow.

"What are you studying . . . Snesia?"

"I like medicine, so I've decided to study for a degree in pharmacy."

Frank's eyes widened. "I'm interested in medicine! In fact, until two years ago, I was a premed student. Now I'm studying for a degree in forestry and wildlife management."

"How interesting," she replied, genuinely interested. "Tell me about your studies."

Frank hardly needed more encouragement. He told her of the

many classes he had taken already—classes that taught park-management theory, wildlife-habitat control, and much more.

Snesia listened closely. "Do you think that you will enjoy being a park manager?"

Frank looked at her, suddenly aware that she had divined his secret. He was in love with the idea of studying outdoor life—the idea of living in the wild among the wild creatures—but he had little concept even now of what a forest ranger did, and if he would enjoy it.

He smiled in reply and shrugged his shoulders helplessly.

Snesia helped him out. "I want to be a pharmacist to help people, to ease suffering. Somehow a job has to be something positive, something that makes the world a better place. I think a job that is concerned with keeping our world fresh and beautiful would also be very rewarding. You'll enjoy it, Frank."

Already he had sensed the incredible idealism of this young Yugoslavian beauty. Perhaps it was part of her naiveté. And yet, she was obviously aggressive in her ambitions. There was already proof enough of that in her ready mastery of English and acceptance of American culture.

Then, too, Snesia's ambition to study pharmacy was not only bold but revolutionary in her case. "I will be the first in my family to graduate from college," she said proudly. "The first as far back as anyone remembers."

The time went by too quickly. Their conversation devoured the brief evening hours.

"I must say goodnight, Frank," said Snesia as the lights around campus began to snap off and the night became even quieter. "It's been wonderful meeting you, and I really enjoyed our talk together."

Frank felt a tug of panic at the thought that this might be it. "When can I see you again?" he asked almost plaintively.

She looked at him with open, trusting eyes. "We can meet again at the club next week if you like."

Too far away, but better than nothing.

"Till next week, then." Suddenly, the urge to reach out and draw her close swept over him. But militarylike discipline took over, and Frank politely extended his hand. Snesia reached out, and their palms touched and gripped in a warm handshake.

"Goodnight, Frank," she smiled, impressed, he imagined, by this display of control.

He watched her as she walked toward her dormitory. In a few short hours, his entire way of thinking had changed. Before, he had been casual around girls and determined to avoid entanglements. Now he was anything but casual and determined to win the affections of this amazingly beautiful girl. Even as the distance between them increased, he felt drawn to her. Something within him cried out to hold her, to protect her. She seemed so young and vulnerable—she needed protection, and he would be her protector.

They met again the next week. Again they talked and discussed many things. Again, they shook hands and said goodbye with promises to meet at the dance club the next week.

By the third meeting, Frank was determined to go beyond a handshake. As they walked away from the gym, he casually put his right arm around Snesia's waist.

Snesia was always full of surprises. To his horror, she took his hand and firmly put it right back at his side. Her Eastern European upbringing had provided her with some clear ideas on familiarity. There were certain conventions to be followed.

In their weekly discussions, the talk often moved to Yugoslavia. Snesia told Frank of the simple village life they had enjoyed there. She also told him of some of their unique customs, such as that of the parents choosing a husband for a daughter. No wonder she was reticent to allow him to hold her. Snesia also made it very clear that she intended to adapt totally to American life—so she wasn't bound by another country's past.

Once more as they walked together, Frank reached across to encircle Snesia's waist with his arm. With seemingly undiminished firmness, she returned his arm to his side. What was he to do?

By their fifth meeting, Frank had determined that he was going to act. He had to do something!

For over an hour, they sat in the gym. The music buoyed up their conversation, and both of them were obviously aware of an increasing attraction. If Snesia were aware of Frank's nervous determination to act in some way, she gave him no hint. She appeared relaxed and happy. Frank was miserable.

With each passing minute, Frank grew more desperate. "I'm going to kiss her tonight," he told himself, only to recoil at the prospect of rejection. He'd muster up new courage. "I am going to kiss her," only to reconsider yet again—"Naw, I'd better not."

Later, beneath a clear, moonlit sky, his resolve returned. Neither felt like talking much as they walked toward the dorm. Frank found it difficult to talk and steel himself for action at the same time. Snesia had her own reasons for being quiet.

Inevitably it was time for goodnights. Snesia held out her hand. "This is it," Frank told himself as he reached and pulled her close by the hand. There was no resistance. The kiss was warm and loving, and Frank knew Snesia cared for him.

Suddenly, the couple found their voices. The tension was broken. Snesia smiled mischievously as they held hands. "Frank, I have to tell you something. Tonight you kissed me for the first time. You know, I had made up my mind that if you didn't kiss me tonight, I was going to stop seeing you."

Frank looked at her incredulously as she continued. "I was beginning to wonder what this kook was hanging around for—just to talk?"

They both laughed, the first of many times, at the buildup to the first kiss. It turned out to be far far from the last one.

From that point on they met twice a week or so. Their activities broadened far beyond the dance club, and they became an "item."

Frank still felt an overwhelming sense of protectiveness toward Snesia. In his eyes she was young and vulnerable. He would protect her and show her in every way that he was a man of honor. He was still very much bound by the codes of honor he had learned at home and at the various Catholic institutions he attended. Something else was at work too. The same steel will, almost an obsession, that Frank applied to his studies and his military exercises showed through in his relationship with Snesia.

He determined to show restraint in the physical side of their relationship. This was mostly a moral choice based on his background. At the same time, deep down, Frank knew that he was actually trying to impress Snesia with his self-discipline—he wanted her to be impressed with him for his refusal to compromise her principles.

Their studies, of course, consumed a great deal of their time and energies. Frank had responsibilities as president of the student co-operative where he lived. The co-op had had a practical side, too, as he needed the money to maintain a certain independence from his parents. At the same time, he continued to lead the raider battalion in commando-style adventures and to participate in regular ROTC training. It was a busy time.

Snesia, too, had a heavy study load, and it made times together difficult to coordinate. Her parents were insistent that she apply herself to the studies, and she did not dare to tell them that she was taking time to meet with Frank. No, they wouldn't understand her involvement with a man they had not met and approved of. Such things were not done in Yugoslavia, in their village.

Despite all the obstacles, however, Frank and Snesia found opportunities to enjoy each other's company. One Sunday, both Frank and Snesia decided they'd had enough of study—time for a break in the nearby park. There was one complication, however. Snesia's parents wanted to come and visit. "No, Mama," Snesia had said when her mother called up to say they were coming. "I have already made plans to study at the library with friends."

Her mother understood such a reason. "Of course, my dear, we would never stand in the way of your schooling. Study hard, and we will visit another time."

It was a lovely, warm day, and the park couldn't have been more pleasant. Frank and Snesia snuggled together in the car, watching all the activity around them. There were several ballgames in progress. A group of small boys played with their model airplanes. Happy family groups picnicked together under the trees, and waterfowl frolicked noisily in the pond near the park entrance.

"Let's go watch the ducks, Frank," Snesia suggested, eager to experience the electric energy of the park.

Hand in hand, they walked toward the pond. Suddenly Snesia stopped in midstep, her face white with fright. "My parents," she half-whispered. "They mustn't see us together." She gestured with her chin to a pleasant-looking couple standing near a car on the other side of the pond. Frank hadn't seen them before. Somehow he felt that this was not the time to meet them.

Quickly they turned and ran for the car. "They'll never forgive me for lying to them if they find out," Snesia blurted. "They mustn't find out."

Frank started the car, and they sped away from the near confrontation. "Oh, Frank, I'm not sorry we met today. My parents have no idea how much I need you." Snesia was shaken, but unrepentant. Frank, too, felt that they were made for each other and had to stay together, no matter the cost.

All too quickly, the months slipped by. It was the second year since their meeting. Snesia was a sophomore with years left ahead of her for the pharmacy accreditation. Frank was close to graduating as a forestry man. How were they to stay in touch after his graduation?

Perhaps it was this uncertainty that led to their discussion one Sunday night at the dorm.

They were both in a carefree mood. Weekends were always a happy, relaxing time, and this one was especially so. After a bit of teasing and clowning around, Frank dropped a suggestion that once spoken, took both their breaths away.

"Wouldn't it be romantic if we were to secretly get married?" he suggested in high spirits. "Think of it. It would be so incredibly bizarre and daring."

"Marry, you!" she mocked lightly. "It would have to be in secret."

"But just think of it, Snesia," Frank pursued the idea; "it would be the most practical way—and the most exciting."

Her face lighted up at the daring of the idea. It appealed to her. "But my parents," Snesia remembered, "they would never agree to it. They still believe in the tradition of the old country. They would never settle for less than the full ceremony—with a man of *their* own choosing."

"All the more reason to go ahead," responded Frank persuasively. "After the fact, what can they do?" As a clincher he added, "We have to act quickly. The year is nearly over, and I'll be leaving. I'm sure to get my notice from the military. We may be apart for years."

"Yes—yes," she said with increasing determination, "let's get married secretly." They sealed their pact with a kiss. It was a romantic notion, and they were both in love.

As soon as he could, Frank contacted a priest. "You'll need two witnesses," the priest said, "and don't forget the civil formalities."

"Civil formalities?" Frank queried. He thought it was just a matter of the priest's blessing.

"You need to get a police clearance, take a blood test, and apply for the marriage certificate," the priest prompted, used to the inexperience of young lovers.

Snesia was already having second thoughts—not about marrying Frank, but new fears about her parent's reaction. "They'll be furious. They'll disown me," she said, voicing her growing concerns. "Maybe we'd better call it off."

Frank saw just how traumatic it was for Snesia to test the ways of her homeland. She needed reassurance.

"Keep calm, Snesia. It's a secret marriage. We can tell them much later when things are calm." He was right in his logic, and Snesia relented.

Snesia went with him to a clinic for the blood tests. She even arranged for two of her friends to join them at the ceremony as witnesses. But at each step she became more fearful, more uncertain.

By Sunday morning Snesia was almost hysterical with apprehension.

Frank, too, had begun to realize the enormity of their independent action. What if Snesia's parents reacted as badly as she feared? Maybe they should call it off, after all.

Then, just when they were about to dismiss all their reservations as foolish, something shocking happened. One of Frank's ROTC buddies called out to them as he passed them in the lobby of the dormitory.

"Hi, lovebirds" was his greeting. "I see you couldn't wait to get hitched."

"What do you mean?" blustered Frank.

"Oh, come on," the friend continued, "it's official—I saw the notice in today's paper."

Frank raced to the newspapers on the coffee table in the lobby. Seizing the Sunday paper, he flipped it through to the announcements section. There it was, in black and white—the announcement of their wedding.

"It was supposed to be secret," wailed Snesia at his shoulder.

"How could they do this to us?" moaned Frank, sure that the whole world had read the notice.

"It's automatic, Buddy," said the friend as he left them to their distress. "There is no way you can stop the public notice."

Snesia cracked. "I can't do it," she exclaimed with sudden determination. "Let's cancel the ceremony. We have to tell my parents we are getting married. We can always set another date for the wedding."

"Yes, you're right," Frank assented, sharing her panic. "I'll call the priest."

He dialed the number with dreamlike precision. "Tell Father Dunston that Frank Kelly and Snesiana Zdravkovich have cancelled their wedding. Thank you." He hung up and looked at Snesia. "It's your turn. Better call before your parents read the notice."

She nodded and dialed the number. When Snesia spoke, it was in rapid, nervous Yugoslavian. Frank understood very little, but he knew what she was telling them.

From several feet away, Frank could hear the angry buzz of Yugoslavian on the other end of the line. Snesia stammered out a little more. There was more angry buzzing and then silence. She put the receiver back on the hook.

"They were furious," she said. "They are driving down here immediately. It will be very bad." Frank noticed that she seemed less shaken than upset—perhaps even angry.

"What did they say?" Frank was almost afraid to ask.

"My father has disowned me." Snesia tried to smile, and bit her lip before continuing. "He said, 'We brought you over to America, and this is what you do to us! Your brother spits on you! We will disown you immediately. Never set foot in this house again!' " She bit her lip again. "He was very upset—I think he means it."

In less time than it should have taken to drive to the university from South Lyon, a car screeched to the curb outside, and the back door swung open.

"Come with me," instructed Snesia, "but say nothing."

They got in the backseat of the car and closed the door to a torrent of angry Yugoslavian. Snesia's father was extremely agitated. He bellowed at the top of his voice. As he looked across at her, never at Frank, he seemed to be propelling the words as missiles to beat down Snesia's defenses. Her mother would add her input from time to time in a softer, but equally desperate, voice.

At one stage Frank was afraid Snesia's father was going to reach back and grab his daughter by the head and shake her like a doll. He was out of his league. He didn't understand what was going on, and he didn't know what to do. Snesia's parents directed all their energies against her. They ignored Frank. In fact, they seemed to be pretending he wasn't there.

Finally Snesia jerked opened the door, and they got out of the car. She slammed it in rage. "I don't care about them," she said. "Let's get married."

Father Dunston was very surprised to get a second call from Frank that Sunday. "The wedding's on," said Frank. "We said it was off, but now it's on."

They were married that same Sunday afternoon. Snesia's two friends changed their schedules a second time and joined them as witnesses.

". . . man and wife," concluded the priest just before Frank and Snesia's first kiss as husband and wife.

Frank looked at the woman he was now joined to by law and the church. She was his snow maiden—nothing would keep them apart now.

"Let's celebrate," he said to Snesia and the witness party of two. "How about going out to eat?"

The two friends were only too happy to share in the moment. They were poor students with little spare money for eating out. The happy meal they shared helped blur the pain of the hours before the wedding. No time to remember the bad. It was a time to celebrate.

After the meal Frank and Snesia said goodbye to their friends and checked into a local motel as Mr. and Mrs. Frank Kelly. It had been so sudden and traumatic, it almost felt illegal!

It was a night of wonder for both of them. They were very much in love. It was, noted Frank, with a lingering pride in his code of honor, their first night together.

The next day they checked out and went back to their classes.

It was still two weeks before the end of the semester and graduation.

That day Frank called his father to break the news of the wedding. He didn't expect as extreme a reaction as that from the Zdravkovichs, but he knew his father would be angry. He had made a point of insisting Frank finish college before getting married. In fact, it had been a sort of promise—almost a condition of his father's financial support.

His father answered the phone in good humor. It wasn't every day his independent second son deigned to check in with him.

"I've called to give you some good news, Dad," Frank announced, hoping to pass it off as something to please the old man.

"Yes." He was just hesitant enough to signal a father's caution. "Have you decided to go back into medicine, Frank?" They both knew that was an unlikely development.

"No, Dad—I just called to let you know that I was married yesterday to the most adorable woman I've ever met." He sped up the last few words in order to finish before the outburst he already sensed.

"You what!" His father was livid with rage. "How dare you go back on your promise? You could have waited till after you graduated. You could have told us you wanted to get married. We don't even know the girl."

"It happened so quickly, Dad," excused Frank. "After all, it is only two weeks until graduation."

Silence.

Now for the clincher. "I couldn't wait, Dad. I already have orders to report to the military. I'm being called up. I couldn't leave Snesia behind."

The voice on the other end was a little calmer. "You broke your word, Son. But what's done is done. Take care of yourself and do the right thing in the military."

That next day the wedding already seemed a little like a beautiful dream of another time and another place.

It was classes as usual. Then there was the ominous call-up notice. In only two weeks, Frank was to report to Fort Belvoir near Washington, D.C., and then on to Fort Campbell, Kentucky. With so little time left, it was impractical to set up house together. For the few days ahead, Frank and Snesia would maintain their separate living quarters.

Snesia was distraught over the split with her family. She cried every night for almost a week.

"Don't cry, Snesia," Frank consoled. "They won't really cut you off, I'm sure."

"You don't know them. You don't know my culture," sobbed Snesia. "They'll never see me again."

"What about your mother, Radmila?" Frank prodded. "Does she love you?"

"Oh, she is the most loving, caring mom anyone could ever have," said Snesia. "But she won't go against my father. I've disgraced him."

"What sort of a man is Milan?" pursued Frank.

"Daddy is soft inside. He was so proud of what I'd accomplished these past few years—his heart must be breaking with disappointment."

"They are good people, and they love you," assured Frank. "It will turn out well in the end, you'll see." He believed what he said, but he had no idea when and how it would all be resolved.

The Friday night after the wedding, the phone rang in Snesia's room. It was Milan and Radmila. Snesia's eyes misted over as she heard her father gruff out the words she later joyously repeated to Frank.

"Look, Snesia, let's forget our little disagreement. You can come back home again any time. Why don't you and Frank come out to dinner with us tonight?"

3

A VERY
PRIVATE WAR

W hat the . . ." the induction-center sergeant was temporarily at a loss for words. He was used to dealing with rebellious young punks. It was his job to bully them into line, and he was good at it. This case was a little different. How was he to deal with a silent one—sitting there with a green plastic bag over his head, no doubt laughing at him under cover of the plastic.

"Now listen here, young man," he bellowed with more than the usual show of belligerence, "get that bag off your head." No answer. "Do you hear me, boy?" No answer from the green one. "What are you, boy, stupid or crazy?" No answer, although the sergeant finally figured he was stupid, and yes, the bright young fellow was out to prove he was crazy—the ultimate excuse to get out of military service.

"Down the hall to your left—door marked 'Psychiatrist'—hop to it," shoved the sergeant, sickened by such ridiculous cowardice.

A long-haired young fellow next to Frank leaned across and nudged him in the ribs. "Talk about weird, man. That's the stupidest excuse I ever saw." Frank had to agree. "Now I've got

31

it all sorted out. You know, I found this doc down in Georgia, and he fixed up my knee real good." Frank looked at his freshly scarred knee, easily visible below the ragged cutoffs. "They'll never take me in the military. No good for long marches, now. I'm out free, man."

These guys were crazy, Frank concluded. Crazily desperate to get out of a war they had no stomach for. Then again, maybe they weren't that mixed up at all. Not nearly as mixed up as his own situation.

It had happened so suddenly he was hardly aware of changing. But somehow in the past few weeks, the whole idea of military service had become distasteful to him. The ROTC had been a game—those middle-of-the-night adventures with the raiders had always belonged to imagination; they had never been real. They certainly had no connection in his mind with the nightly news reports of horror in Vietnam and the political cynicism that prolonged the killing. He was against the war and against the military machine.

Only a few days earlier, Snesia had clung to him in fear of Vietnam. "Don't go, Frank," she implored. "You must not go to Vietnam. I need you."

There was one way out. He had discovered that if he signed up for an extra year of service he could request the station of his choice. Germany seemed the logical alternative. Snesia agreed. Anything to keep her Frank away from Vietnam. Anything to keep him safe.

It was an almost unbearably painful decision for Frank to make. He would willingly have paid $2,000 or even $3,000 to escape military service. He envied those who used family political influence to avoid Vietnam. Watching the plastic-bag case grope down the hall toward a psychiatric excuse, Frank somehow envied him. He stood to beat the system. Frank was giving in to the system and signing away an extra year of his life.

He was ordered to report to Fort Belvoir, near Washington, D.C., for six months of specialized training. It was a long way from Michigan, but at least he would have Snesia with him. It would be their first chance to set up house together. Snesia could continue her studies while he endured the military.

There were a lot of other military couples in the apartment

building they eventually chose. Plenty of wives for Snesia to socialize with while the husbands spent the days practicing for
war.

Frank and Snesia quickly struck up an easy friendship with a
couple a few doors down from their apartment. Neal and Jenny
Isabelle became their closest friends. In fact, Frank and Neal
were united by a particularly common bond—they both felt that
the army was a total pile of foolishness. They were both taking
the same basic courses at the base and were both determined to
frustrate the system.

"Let's really show them that we are not part of the ridiculous
charade," suggested Neal when they first compared attitudes.
"Let's do everything we can to fight the indoctrination."

"It's sure to go badly for us, Neal," suggested Frank, still in
agreement with the basic idea.

"So what!" Neal responded. "About the worst they can do is
discharge us." He had a point.

"Let's see who will be the lowest-rated in our class. It'll take
some doing, but I know I'll be the one." Neal saw it as a challenge.

"I hate this scene as much as you, Neal. Maybe I'll beat you to
the bottom." Frank was in on the dare. It would shape their
military experience for the months ahead.

In very short order Frank and Neal developed a reputation as
two of the sloppiest, most uncooperative soldiers on the base.

Neal nearly clinched the bet during grenade practice. Frank
watched his performance in amazed admiration.

The initial drill was done using dummy grenades. Neal and
Frank sat on the benches at the grenade range and listened to
the sergeant go over the basics.

"Hold the grenade firmly—like this," he boomed. "Then pull
the pin, wait for the count, and then throw it high and forward."
He picked up a dummy grenade. "Now watch once more—like
this." The grenade floated in a high arc, well out onto the range.

"Isabelle," he ordered, "come and show us how it's done."

"Watch this," whispered Neal as he moved past Frank. Maybe
he was going to go for a distance record. Frank remembered Neal
telling him that he'd played a lot of softball in school.

"Hold the grenade firmly," instructed the sergeant as Neal

casually picked up a dummy. "Now move forward firmly and lob it out ahead of you." Neal swung the grenade in a wide arc and released. It flew backwards out of his hand, into the bench area.

"Once more, soldier," barked the sergeant impatiently.

Again Neal swung and released. The grenade rose gracefully straight into the air. Both Neal and the sergeant backed off as it plummeted down.

"Very clever, soldier," snapped the sergeant, sure of a setup now. "Try it next time with a live grenade."

Neal looked across at Frank and winked as he and the sergeant walked over to the concrete bunker. Once there he pulled the pin from the grenade with a slow, deliberate action. For a long moment he held the grenade, then with a loose, casual motion lobbed it about two feet in front of the bunker.

The sergeant panicked. Inside the bunker was a little hole leading to a chamber in the floor. It was there as a last resort should a primed grenade land in the bunker. The idea was to throw the grenade down the hole, where it would explode relatively harmlessly. The sergeant leapt at that hole and tried to force himself inside. With a roar the grenade exploded against the outer concrete wall. Everyone was pretty shaken up. Neal, of course, looked pleased with himself.

Neal got into a lot of trouble for that stunt. Naturally, the sergeant ripped him up and down with choice, unprintable insults. But interestingly, the worst came from the other recruits. Already the peer-pressure system was honed to a cutting edge, and they virtually ostracized Neal for daring to go against the military machine.

Frank found the peer-pressure routine intolerable. First, there was the case of the party organized by the graduates of military colleges. Of course, everybody was expected to attend and to contribute to the fund. Frank and Neal and one other brave fellow would not go along.

A few days before the party an officer read off the names of those who hadn't contributed. He read the list to the entire class. The intent was to disgrace them in front of their peers. It failed. Frank and Neal stood proudly as they were named for not paying. It was an open expression of their rebellion, and others took note of it. Most condemned them as troublemakers; a few secretly envied their willingness to stand up and go against the group opinion.

A second major aggravation to Frank was the practice whereby each recruit had to sit down and rate who was top of the class and who was bottom of the class. Every one of the hundred or so men in their group was asked to do this, and Frank found it intolerable.

It was about then that Frank was selected to go with a representative group of trainees for a meeting with the base commander. It was designed to be very informal. Respectfully, the group sat down with the general and discussed nonthreatening issues over drinks and a light snack.

This was Frank's big chance.

"General," he said, "you know, I am really upset about this peer-review program." The general's eyebrows shot up in surprise at his bluntness. Frank cast caution aside and continued. "It smacks of Communism, in my estimation. In Russia everyone reports on his brother, mother, and father. And here we are, forced to do the same sort of thing. I don't like this system at all."

The general took it very badly. "This is the military, son," he chided. "Our system depends on knowing your fellow soldiers and knowing you can rely on them." The inference was clear. Question the system too much, and you'll be known as a traitor.

Afterwards, those students anxious to please the general came to Frank and criticized him for daring to compare the military system to Communism.

"It's a ridiculous comparison, Kelly," blustered one of them. "Nothing to do with Communism. This is America—don't try to say that peer review here has anything to do with Communism. You're a troublemaker."

Frank found the logic of their reply somewhat lacking. He was even more disturbed to learn that the general was proud of the group for condemning him. From that point on he was convinced that the whole system was rotten. He couldn't wait to get out.

Frank's change of mind went beyond a new perspective on military life. He had been brought up to respect and obey the dictates of his parent's church. Neal Isabelle was a real catalyst for change in that area too.

Even at the university Frank made a point of regularly attending mass. It was a habit drummed into him through the years at McQuaid Jesuit High School and Loyola College. Those habits died hard. The training had been persistent and persuasive. If he were to disregard the church, his very soul would be in danger. It was unthinkable.

His marriage to Snesia had been a rebellion of sorts. It cut the last ties of obligation to his family. But it actually underscored his devotion to the church. The wedding was a wild, crazy idea— but it was inconceivable without the offices of a priest. Frank needed the security of knowing the church was behind him.

Snesia did not share his reverence for the Catholic Church. She had no particular arguments against it. Rather, she had an all-embracing disbelief that probably came from the way she had moved on from all the reminders of old Yugoslavia. This was America, where you chose your own destiny. So what if there were nothing beyond this dream?

Every Sunday, Frank took the time to go to services and mass. It seemed the right thing to do. Every Sunday he climbed onto his bicycle and pedaled across for what amounted to weekly penance.

One Sunday morning after the mass, Frank discovered that his bike was gone—stolen from right in front of the church. Almost a sacrilege! He stomped over the seemingly longer distance back to the apartment, full of dark feelings about people who hung around churches and stole bicycles.

"Hello, Frank." It was Neal who called to him outside the apartment. "How did it go at mass this morning?"

Neal was dressed in his Sunday best, too, and Frank guessed that Neal had just returned from services at the nearby Baptist church that he attended.

"Mass was the same as usual. The crazy thing is someone stole my bicycle."

Neal looked sympathetic.

"Maybe it's a sign of sorts that you should not go to mass anymore," he suggested, almost as a joke.

"Not go to church? My parents would never forgive me," said Frank, "and the priest would hardly approve. He would expect to see me at confession for some sort of explanation."

Neal looked at Frank with something approaching pity. "Oh, don't be that afraid of the consequences. You might find that your old church has been fooling you a bit—just like you were fooled by the military."

That made sense to Frank. He could still remember those simple days in the drill team and with the raiders when he thought that nothing could be more honorable than military life.

"I used to be a Catholic, Frank." Neal had never told him that before. "Yes, I grew up in Catholic institutions and went through the usual brainwashing."

"What do you mean?" quizzed Frank.

"You must remember it. Learning the catechism, repeating the mass, listening to the horrible fate of all those who reject church teaching."

Actually, Frank had been giving a lot of thought to such things lately.

"Yes, I can remember the nuns scaring the socks off me by outlining the punishment of those in limbo or hell. The nuns encouraged us to give up things—to sacrifice ourselves for the church—and the more they talked about it, the more impossible it seemed."

"But they kept at you." Neal nodded.

"Yes. They made me believe that just thinking of a swear word was sin and I was in mortal danger until I confessed to them."

"I remember the same thing," added Neal.

"It all seemed so religious at the time," mused Frank, "but looking back on it I can see that it was unhealthy. For example, I can vividly remember how the nun's exhortations led me to some pretty obsessive behavior at Lent."

"Me too," concurred Neal, aware that the scales were dropping from Frank's eyes.

"During that period I chose seventy of the most popular tortures for myself. It was obsessive, and the nuns encouraged me even suggested it to me."

Neal shook his head slowly in a sign of disgust.

"For those forty days I had no candy bars, no desserts, or other things far more necessary. It got to the point of almost no meals. I was sleeping on the floor at night and getting up in the morning to splash cold water in my face. It was self-flagellation—and the church smiled. It is frightening when I look back on it."

"Brainwashing," said Neal suddenly, and they both laughed to relieve the tension.

"Yes, it's so obvious now, but at the time I fell for it," lamented Frank.

"Just like you fell for the idea that the pope is some sort of divine leader—a leader who can trace his position in an unbroken line to Peter."

Frank's eyes narrowed at such a basic questioning of his church's claims.

"Why, the pope can no more prove his descent from the leadership of Peter than you can. Peter was just one of the apostles who led the early Christian church. There is no evidence he was given special or sole authority over the church."

"Go on," encouraged Frank, wanting to hear more.

"All the major church centers had bishops or leaders in the years following the death of the apostles. But by the end of the first century, there was still no bishop to lead the church in Rome. Of course, with or without that fact, there could be no succession of absolute spiritual authority, as a clear reading of the Bible makes plain and the writings of others from that time confirm."

"So how did the pope come to claim total authority?" puzzled Frank.

"It happened as a direct result of the emperor Constantine embracing Christianity as the state religion for the Roman Empire. This was in the third century A.D. Naturally, the bishop of Rome, the capital of the empire, gained a lot of prestige and power in the religious world. Then as the power of the emperors diminished with the disintegration of the empire, the bishops of Rome assumed a secular power as well. By the fifth century A.D., they were solidly entrenched as a papal power."

"Yes, I know you are right," assented Frank. "I've read the history of the papacy, and it just doesn't add up to what the church claims. It amounts to a monumental and pretentious lie."

"And then look at what this Christian church has done to any group or person that challenged its absolute authority," suggested Neal.

More history, thought Frank, with a full realization of the record of the inquisition, the papal wars against "heretics," and the continuing enmity toward Protestant breakaways. "Not a pretty picture, I guess," he finished lamely. It was over. All the questions on his mind, so long simmering, so long put down by piety, came to the boiling point.

"I believe in God," he said defensively as though Neal had challenged him. "But I'm done with the Catholic Church."

Neal looked sympathetic. "Why not come along with me to the Baptist church next week?" he suggested.

"Do the Baptists have it all together?" asked Frank, more to hear Neal's response than needing any proof.

"I'm not really sure yet," admitted Neal with the candor of close friendship. "But I've found they are pretty basic with the Bible on most things."

"You told me you used to go to a Pentecostal church," prodded Frank.

"Well, yes," admitted Neal. "It's just that something was missing there too. I really got into the speaking in tongues, but somehow it all seemed a bit gory. Lately I've been giving the Baptists a try."

"Let's both try the Baptist church next week," determined Frank.

And he was as good as his suggestion. Frank worshiped at the Baptist church for several weeks in a row. He enjoyed the chance to continue a worship of God, but he felt no overriding compulsion to join their congregation. Maybe it was Neal. He was a good friend. He could debunk Catholicism with the best of them. The only problem was, he didn't live the answer. Frank could see that Neal himself was still searching. After Catholicism, Pentecostalism, Methodism, and the Baptist Church were just stopping points for Neal. Frank needed to find the destination for himself.

Frank had originally expected to spend only six months in training at Fort Belvoir. As always, his inquiring nature got the better of him, and he signed up for a six-month extension course in topography. Some of the classes reminded him of his forestry studies, and he found the course a real challenge.

Both Frank and Neal were still bothered by the unholy bargain they had struck with the army—an extra year in the service in exchange for posting to the country of their choice.

On one occasion Neal was so moved to dissent that he leaped to his feet during a class discussion and ranted against the policy. "The idea of spending another year in this army is so intolerable I would rather go to Vietnam instead." He hardly intended to follow up on the alternative, but it was a great way to voice his frustration. By this time he knew that a lot of the others agreed with him in their hearts. But he didn't care about the generalized snickers in the class as he sat down to a pat on the back from Frank. The two of them were way out in left field and careless of the consequences.

Whatever his real thoughts about the military, Frank knew he would have to play the game if he were to land a good posting to Germany. He determined that he would apply to the topographical battalion at Oftersheim, near Heidelberg. It was one of only two such groups in Germany at the time.

He wrote letters. He feigned a great interest in assisting the military machine in that sphere. And somehow, someone overlooked his private war with the army. When the assignments were posted, he was one of thirty-six students accepted for Oftersheim.

The bad part of this news was saying goodbye to Snesia. She was still studying toward her degree in pharmacology, and it seemed pointless for her to waste the time by breaking off mid-semester.

She saw him off at the airfield. They both knew it wouldn't be more than four months before the semester ended and they'd be together again. That didn't keep the tears away for Snesia.

"Promise you'll write, Frank," she implored.

"Of course, Snesia. How could I ever forget the love of my life?" He tried to make it sound casual, but actually, he, too, felt it was a big moment.

"At least I'm heading to Europe," he reminded her. "It could have been Vietnam."

They kissed like newlyweds again, and he was off, his kit bag slung purposefully over his for once neatly pressed dress uniform. He was no grunt—he was a lieutenant, an officer in the U.S. Army, off to conquer new worlds. And too young to realize he didn't really know the first thing about military life.

His education began the day he arrived at Oftersheim.

Once through the front gates, he headed straight to the main office. A big, hulking black sergeant was busy talking on the phone. It turned out he was a thirty-year veteran who had dealt with more than a few new arrivals.

"Sergeant," brazened Frank, in what he meant to be an air of authority, "give me my desk right now."

The sergeant's eyes barely flicked up at him. He gave no sign of having seen Frank, and kept talking on the phone. Finally, after several minutes had passed, he lay down the receiver and looked at Frank as though he were a mosquito that had somehow flown into the room.

He rose indifferently and walked through to the company commander. Frank heard his comment quite clearly. "Sir," he said, "#*!**# has just arrived." Frank blushed at his title. Also, he still hadn't figured out why his command didn't work. Frank thought that officers gave commands. It took him a while to figure out that only the privates took much notice of his commands—and even some of them told him where to get off.

Maybe it was because he had such a time adjusting to the reality of military life that he let up a bit on his letters to Snesia. Actually, he wasn't aware of any special delay—it was just that the initial routine left him so bamboozled, he kept putting off the letters. He made the big mistake of not writing her for three weeks.

Then he started getting letters. Other women were writing to him! They weren't admirers, however. All of them were friends of Snesia, and they pretty much gave the same message. "What are you trying to do, Frank, drive your wife to desperation? She is frantic with worry and uncertainty. She looks bad, Frank. We are afraid she's near a physical breakdown just from worrying."

Thoroughly repentant, Frank dashed off a number of letters. In fact he sent something like five letters a day hoping to make amends. Then he got a letter back from Snesia—she was satisfied.

Shortly after that, Snesia arrived in Germany. The letter-writing episode was over, and they set up house again, honeymoon style.

Things may have calmed down on the home front, but the war was heating up for Frank on base. Every regulation, every order rose up as a challenge, and Frank fought them all.

By now he was thoroughly in sympathy with the anti-war movement. In his estimation the Vietnam War was a politician's war, and he would not support it in any way. The other officers learned to steer clear of him. They pretty much ostracized him for his generally insubordinate attitude. His superiors found him openly uncooperative, but somehow they couldn't get the right regulations together to discipline him.

Frank made no effort to hide his disdain for the army. On one occasion the base commander stopped by for a chat, hopeful that a sympathetic ear might be all Frank needed.

"Good to see you today, Lieutenant Kelly," beamed the commander, a genuinely easy-natured sort, who liked to think of his officers as junior members of a family. "How goes the war?"

It was a poor image to present to an increasingly frustrated Lieutenant Kelly.

"The war goes badly, . . . sir!" retorted Frank, his intention of a larger meaning all too clear.

"Well, Frank, just console yourself with the fact that this base is carrying out its responsibilities just fine. Keep waving that flag, boy."

"It's no good, sir. We are a part of the same corrupt machinery that's run amok in Vietnam."

The commander blinked at his vehemence.

Frank went on, pushing his disadvantage to the limit. "Actually, sir, I think the army is nothing more than Murder Incorporated."

"In the future you'll do well to keep such opinions to yourself," warned the base commander, fixed now in his opinion of Frank Kelly as a troublemaker.

It wasn't just the big issues that troubled Frank. He was equally rattled by the myriad of rules and regulations that seemed so pointless and were so rigorously enforced.

Like the time the security officer came into Frank's office and asked him to follow army regulations and secure the number of the safe in the room. It was standard policy, but it seemed so ridiculous.

"Just do it," directed the security officer. "Write down the number of your safe, put it in an envelope, put that envelope inside a larger envelope, and then staple it shut. Then give it to me, and I'll put it in the main base safe." Why, he even had trouble saying it himself. A real boy-scout game if ever there were one.

"Why don't you come in here and write it down yourself?" Frank demanded, rebelling at the idea.

Amazingly, he did, probably thinking it would humble Frank into completing the procedure. Frank took the envelope from him and began to staple it shut. He stapled until there was no more room on the envelope to punch in even one more staple— hundreds of staples—they probably weighed eight ounces or so.

He took the heavy and unrecognizable envelope back to the security officer.

"Put this in your safe," he challenged. The officer sneered "Lieutenant Kelly" through clinched teeth to show he despised him.

Neal Isabelle wound up at another base in Germany working on maintenance and base construction. He and Frank made contact from time to time, and it was obvious that Frank was the one striking the most sparks of discontent. The way things had begun at Fort Belvoir, Frank expected Neal to wind up being booted out of the military. Surprisingly, that never happened. Neal sailed through his tour in Germany, returned to the States, and, in order to avoid doing his four years of reserve duty, moved every four months or so. In a practical sense the army put his life on hold and got the better of him.

Meanwhile at Oftersheim, Frank was lashing out in ever more petty ways. Sometimes he wondered why they let him loose in the place, as he did his best to foul things up.

There was the time when as officer of the day he decided to liven things up a bit the next day. He took the deluxe electric typewriter belonging to the colonel's secretary and swapped it for the old Remington on the supply clerk's desk. He knew it would create confusion and jealousy the next day. He was right.

First thing the supply clerk noticed the next morning was the typewriter. "Oh, my stars," he exclaimed, "I have a new typewriter." And off he went to tell the others in the office.

Then the colonel's secretary saw his new typewriter. "What the dickens is going on here?" he sputtered. It took a long time to sort things out and smooth ruffled feathers. After all, it wasn't just a question of typewriters, it was a matter of status.

If they suspected Frank, no one said. But it was difficult to overlook his obvious pleasure at the mixup.

It got to the point where Frank felt under no obligation to make any pretense of carrying out his job in a reasonable manner. When the telephone rang, he would pick it up and drop it back into the cradle—no matter how often it rang. In fact, he was sabotaging the operation from within. He couldn't get away with it forever.

One evening Frank arrived home with a funny smile on his face. Snesia had to guess what his news was. She tried, but none of the questions came close, according to Frank.

"Great news, Honey," he revealed at last. "I flunked my efficiency report—for the second time."

She looked at him blankly.

"It means," he leaned forward, "that they finally got me. That I'm free. After thirteen months in Germany, I'm free to go home—discharged."

Snesia still looked at him uncomprehendingly.

"Don't you understand? Flunking an efficiency report twice is automatic discharge. It's not a dishonorable discharge. The only attachment is I'm not allowed to do my four years service in the reserves—*big deal!*"

By now Snesia was smiling broadly herself. Now they could get back to their real lives in the U.S. "I'll write my parents that we'll see them soon," she exulted. "They'll be so happy to see us."

Frank had one parting item to share regarding the discharge. "Actually, I served with rather unique distinction. They tell me that only two second lieutenants have ever been kicked out this way—being barred from automatic promotion. Only two—myself and some fellow back in the Civil War."

Snesia couldn't help herself and was already on the phone dialing South Lyon, Michigan. Frank let her call. This was one call he would not slam down into the cradle.

"We're coming home," Snesia began excitedly in Yugoslavian. "The war is over." And Frank knew exactly what she meant. It was over.

4

AN OUTDOOR
JOB

*T*he key turned slowly, uncertainly in the lock. Snesia heard it click, followed by the irregular creak of the door hinges. It was Frank, back later than she'd expected him.

"Any luck, Frank?" she called out as he made his way to the lounge and slumped down in the easy chair.

He didn't feel like talking.

"How did the job hunting go, Frank?" Snesia never took No—or in this case, silence—for an answer.

"I applied for another forestry job," he began somewhat redundantly. They both knew that he had been trying to land a forestry job for weeks now.

"Would you believe it? Three hundred and fifty people applied for one lousy forestry job. Three hundred and fifty! This administration's austerity program has gone too far. The way the forestry program has been cut back, there will never be enough jobs to go around. Never!"

"So you didn't get the job?" Snesia didn't much care for self-pity. "There's always tomorrow. You'll get a forestry job soon."

"No." Frank shook his head. "No, it's just not worth beating my head against the wall anymore. For all practical purposes there are no forestry jobs. Not anymore."

"So what will you do?" Snesia was aggravated by the admission of failure she sensed.

"Well, actually, I have a job," Frank brightened. "I've signed up to work on a construction outfit as a work supervisor." He saw the gathering storm in his lady's eyes and continued quickly, "It pays well, and we need money pretty badly. Remember, there's food, rent, and your tuition to pay—you've got to continue your pharmacy studies. You need to keep pushing away at the degree." Snesia nodded the agreement of one overachiever to another.

"Actually, it may turn out to be an interesting job," Frank continued. "The construction firm I'm joining specializes in power plants."

"And where are they building now?" Snesia asked, suddenly guessing that the job might require them to move from Michigan.

"I'll be working at Bay City, Michigan," reassured Frank. "Don't worry, we'll still be able to visit your folks whenever we want."

And in a way, life did take on a sort of normalcy for Frank and Snesia in the following few years. They set up house again, argued a lot, tested each other's patience, made up a lot, and grew together in many shared experiences. Snesia continued her pharmacy studies, and Frank almost enjoyed his responsibilities as a work supervisor and civil engineer.

But the inevitable finally happened. Power plants, even very big ones like the one at Bay City, eventually get built; the turbines start turning, and the workers move on. Frank decided to stay with the company and move on to the next project—construction of what was to be the largest coal-burning generator in the country.

"Shipping Port," Frank told Snesia when she asked about the new job. "Shipping Port, Pennsylvania," he added rather superfluously. Snesia already knew they would be leaving Michigan.

As they drove the tree-lined miles to Pennsylvania, Frank had time again to reflect on the irony of his situation. He was trained in forestry management, conditioned for the outdoor life, and now seemingly locked into the mechanical grind of industry, an industry that essentially depended on destruction of trees and the environment. It even crossed his mind as the miles sped away that the practice of medicine might be no farther away from his forestry ideal than the power-plant assignment.

Once in Pennsylvania, Snesia resumed her studies. She was a good student but an erratic one. She had a natural aptitude and quick mind. Still, she hated to study. Sometimes it seemed to Frank that without him, Snesia might just quit the course. But she never did, in spite of much complaining and threatening. They fought their way through her various courses and fell deeper in love for the shared conflict.

The real conflict was something Frank kept locked up inside. He felt trapped. He needed to reach out, to try the adventure of life—to escape the press of civilization and technology.

Each day Frank worked on the power plant, he felt the oppression more deeply. Like a growing tower of Babel, the power-plant stack grew monolithically to its eventual 900-foot height. It flared outward at the top and seemed to threaten his world with imminent collapse. At times, it cast such a huge shadow over the landscape that Frank saw it as a symbol of all the gloomy frustrations in his life. He had to escape somehow.

The very first time he heard the name of the outdoor club, Frank felt he had found the answer to his unease. The Explorers Club of Pittsburg! Now that was a ticket to adventure, if anything was.

At first Snesia found his enthusiasm unsettling. "Exploring!" She huffed, "Why would I want to go exploring, Frank? I like it just fine around town. There's plenty to do here. We can have good times in the city you know. I don't need to rough it."

"You don't understand," Frank continued calmly the first time they discussed it. "The club offers all sorts of outdoor expertise and activities. It's not just a club for rough adventures but a social gathering of people who share an interest in the active life." He was used to Snesia's stubbornness by now and took her objections in stride. She was sure to come around.

"Just think of all the fascinating activities they offer, Snesia," he continued persuasively. "Expert club members will teach us kayaking, rafting, hang gliding, parachuting, scuba diving, vertical caving, hiking, mountaineering, ice climbing, rock climbing, windsurfing, and skiing!" He paused for breath and to remember some of the many other activities the club sponsored. He opted to go for the basics in his sales pitch. "Look, Snesia, honey, we've been through some rough-and-tumble times together, some real good times too. I think that if we take up some of these activities together it will help our marriage." She smiled. They were in the club.

From that point on, their weekends and holidays were totally taken up with one outdoor adventure after another. In winter it was downhill skiing at any number of nearby resorts. Frank found the downhill skiing exciting enough, but soon concluded that telemark skiing was for him. He took special pride in struggling down a steep slope on the thin, unstable cross-country skis. Both he and Snesia enjoyed the stamina-building exercise of a brisk cross-country ski jaunt. Other times they joined club members on dangerous excursions to ice cliffs and snow-covered mountains. Frank enjoyed the adrenalin rush of these adventures in survival. Snesia was a little more cautious, but at Frank's prompting she went along.

In the warmer months there were other outings to such places as the White Mountains of New Hampshire and Seneca Rocks in West Virginia—a mecca for rock climbing on the East Coast.

Working at the power plant, Frank felt threatened by the looming man-made rock wall of the huge concrete smokestack. But he was drawn to natural rock faces like Seneca Rocks. The rocks were not especially steep, but they were tricky in spots and a real challenge. Many times, Frank and Snesia went to Seneca Rocks for a weekend of rock climbing and kayaking in the nearby white-water rapids. And always, Frank felt the fascination of the place.

The very first time they struggled up the rock face with an Explorers Club team, Frank noticed the distinctive shape of the rocks. He called his question up to the team leader. "Hey, Gary, what do you think of the shape of these rocks—those three humps at the top that almost look like giant figures watching us climb?"

"You're not the first one to see figures in the rocks; the Indians had a legend to go with the three shapes."

Frank and the others paused a moment as Gary told the story

of an Indian chief, his wife, and their daughter—the three stone figures.

"The Indian girl's name was Snow Bird," continued Gary. Frank and Snesia exchanged knowing glances. Snesia was a snow girl too—her name meant Snow White, or snow maiden.

"The legend goes this way. Snow Bird climbed the rocks, pursued by all the young braves of the tribe. The first one to the top would claim her as his bride.

"Well, the rocks were steep, and the braves fell before they reached the top. But, finally one brave made it all the way— almost. Just as he reached for the top edge he slipped and fell back. He would have met the fate of the others, but Snow Bird reached out and pulled him up to safety."

"Smart girl," breathed Snesia, her hands tightly gripping the climbing rope that linked her to Frank and the members of the group.

"I'll never feel comfortable with this rock-climbing business," Snesia called down to Frank, "never." One hand on the rope and the other wedged in a crevice above her head, she pulled herself upward awkwardly, her feet scrambling for a grip on the smooth rock face.

"Sure you will, honey," reassured Frank from below. He just loved the challenge of the climb. Somehow Snesia had to learn to share that feeling. It would give them more common interests and help their marriage—he was sure of it.

Too bad, though, that Snesia showed such little aptitude on the rocks. She was athletic enough—she regularly ran long distances and was fit enough to outwalk most of the male hikers in the club. Her long, slim legs were trim and the muscles taut. But somehow she was awkward on the rocks. *I hope she gets over it,* Frank thought to himself. *Maybe she just needs practice. No danger, though,* he consoled himself. With the climbers securely roped together, a fall would be more embarrassing than dangerous.

After the climb the club members sat around sharing the day's experiences and plotting future outings for other days and other places. It was a time of warm camaraderie.

"You guys should join up with John Irving's expedition to the Santa Maria Mountains in Colombia," suggested Gary enthusiastically. "John is a real adventurer, and any outing he plans will be memorable."

Snesia looked interested. She liked traveling. Frank seized on the moment to ask more. "When does the expedition leave?" he wanted to know.

"Oh, plenty of time yet," assured Gary. "They'll leave around December next year. Lots of time to plan and save for the trip," he added persuasively.

"How difficult will the climbing be?" pursued Frank. "After all, we are not yet up to the Hillary level." He still remembered Snesia's awkwardness on the rocks. *Mustn't rush her with too big a challenge*, he thought.

"Don't worry about being outclassed on the climb, Frank," was the easy reply.

"John is a very experienced climber and leader. I know that several of the people already planning to go are raw beginners. John will adjust his plans to their skills." Frank relaxed a little. "What's more, the Santa Marias are only baby peaks—about 19,000 feet!" Frank tensed again, but with anticipation this time. It would be a great challenge and a great adventure. They had to go.

Flushed with her victory over the Seneca Rocks, Snesia shared his taste for adventure. "Sure, why not, Frank?" she concurred with his thoughts. "Let's plan on going. I can take the time to go on the trip."

"But your studies . . ." remembered Frank.

"You've gotten too used to my struggling with my studies," Snesia chided somewhat triumphantly. "It's almost over. By the end of next year I'll have completed my pharmacy studies."

Frank looked at her, wide-eyed and smiling. "How about we go climb some hills in Colombia?" he asked. "After all, we'll be free as birds by then."

Whatever freedom they looked forward to, however, was spoiled by what had promised to be a great adventure. The Colombia expedition was a disaster. The weather had turned sour on the group and so had tempers. John, the climb leader, had turned out to be reckless and unsympathetic to the less-experienced climbers on the team. Heated words were exchanged, and fisticuffs were only narrowly averted.

By the time the dispirited adventurers reached the States again, there were enough lighter moments, enough minor troubles of other sorts, to dull the anger a little. They had shared the miseries of dysentery, seen lessons in poverty, and discovered other memories of a foreign land that covered, and, indeed, compensated for the trauma in the mountains.

Back in Pittsburg, Frank resumed his job at the power plant. Snesia, now an accredited pharmacist, landed a plum job at a nearby Veteran's Administration hospital and was soon managing their out-patient area. The frustrations in Colombia notwithstanding, both Frank and Snesia remained committed to the outdoor life and the Explorers Club. They had many adventures yet to experience.

5

DIRECTIONS

G reat place, Frank, old buddy." The music was loud—almost too loud to hear anything with certainty. But the raised glass of beer and beaming face of his boss filled in the details. Frank smiled and watched the man swill down another glass. The bar reeked of stale beer, and the heavy cloud of cigarette smoke stung his eyes in constant reminder of how much he hated the whole scene.

"Well, Frankie boy," the man slurred as he gave Frank's shoulder an amiable drunken slap, "I've got my eye on you, that's for sure. You'll go far in the company, and I'll see to it that you get the breaks you deserve."

Frank took the slap and the alcohol-induced endorsement with superficial appreciation. Inside he was churning. He hated the routine demanded for advancement in the power-plant construction company. He knew it so well by now. Take the boss out for beer every day, get drunk with him—or at least get him drunk, tell a few stories, slap each other on the back, drop a few hints about work aspirations, and then wait for the man to promise a promotion. For a vacation he might take a supervisor out to a ballgame. They'd shout themselves hoarse, dunk a few tinnies, and, again, talk of advancement at work—man to man, one sports fan to another—buddies.

It was a demeaning, hypocritical routine and Frank hated it. He wanted to get ahead in life, in his job, but not this way, and not that badly.

Even as he raised his glass to his smiling supervisor, he knew that tomorrow the man would respond just as easily to whichever of Frank's rivals in lower management was willing to spring for the day's beerfest. Backbiting and backstabbing were operative words in the company struggle for advancement.

"Not for me," Frank told himself for perhaps the hundredth time. But this time he intended to act on it.

"Well, get out of the company if that's really how you feel about it," Snesia answered when he repeated his frustration that night. "Why stick with it when you hate it so much?"

Snesia had a direct, no-nonsense way of looking at difficult situations. She was right, of course, and Frank was in just the frame of mind to act. A forestry career was still an impossible dream, but in recent months he had been toying with another alternative.

"I may go back to school," he stated by way of gauging Snesia's reaction.

It was positive. "That's a good idea, Frank," she affirmed. "You supported me all those years while I was studying. I'll support you while you go back to school and study."

So it was agreed. Back to school. But what was he to study?

Frank hesitated for a moment before he spoke. It was an announcement he had stifled for years. "I'm going back to school to study medicine!"

Snesia didn't seem surprised. Her "Why?" was more in the way of asking him to vocalize the reasons she'd already guessed at.

"I guess I've matured a bit over the years, Snesia." He knew that was the biggest change. Now he no longer saw medicine as a profession that would imprison him within four walls of a dull consulting room. He had come to realize that a doctor could choose his own niche in life—serve in the area that suited his temperament and skills. Maybe he'd picked up that insight from outdoor club expeditions with fellow adventurers—doctors his own age. More likely, it had come as a natural consequence of maturity and an awareness that not only was he not bound by the aspirations of his parents but that those aspirations just might be the best for him.

They accepted him at Hahneman Medical School, Philadelphia. "You're a bit older than our usual applicant," commented the registrar as he approved Frank's application. "However, your grades during your first two years of premed were quite high, and—"

"And I will keep them high here at Hahneman," countered Frank. He liked the challenge. In a way it was like climbing a mountain. He had to get to the top, no matter what.

"Yes, I think you will," agreed the registrar, looking over the results of the entrance exam. "Good luck in the next four years of study, and welcome to Hahneman." He was in!

It didn't take long to arrange the move down to Philadelphia. Very quickly Snesia found employment at the nearby Veteran's Administration hospital. Frank began his studies in high spirits. The future looked bright and his dreams unlimited.

Almost immediately he linked up with the University of Pennsylvania Outdoor Club. They were a great group, confident and aggressive, with lots of exciting plans for year-round adventures. Frank and Snesia joined them for many outings. Caving in West Virginia, hiking in New Hampshire, and cross-country skiing in New York.

Jack Vance, an English teacher at the university and a member of the club, was an expert in rock climbing. He and Frank hit it off from the start. They were both adventurous types. Both enjoyed the danger of climbing and the challenge of a high rock face. So it was only natural that they joined forces and ran a rock-climbing class for students at the medical school.

Snesia as always was a little uncomfortable with the rock-climbing side of their outdoor adventures. "It's dangerous, Frank," she exclaimed over and over, whenever the talk touched the subject.

"But so much of what we do is dangerous," countered Frank, well aware that Snesia was a little awkward and uncoordinated on the rocks, despite her high level of physical fitness.

"That's what my parents keep saying," she pointed out. "They live in constant fear that something will happen to us—to me."

"I know," agreed Frank. "They do try to lay a guilt trip on me for taking you on our adventures. They don't quite understand the skill and training that go into a safe adventure."

"But it isn't always safe, is it, Frank?" Snesia prodded. "Remember the ledge in Colombia."

Would he ever forget that tight spot!

At this point in the conversation, like so many times before, they both acknowledged the danger and the consequences.

"Yes, we might die in an accident," Frank would say, "but at least we'll have lived life to the full. We've already had adventures that many only dream about."

It was worth the risk, they agreed. In fact, both of them expected to be killed in an accident before long. They both expected it to be themselves; the other spouse would be all right.

Snesia was particularly philosophical about the possibility. "If I die, that's the end of it," she maintained. "There's nothing beyond this comedy."

Frank always found her attitude disturbing. He was no longer committed to his parent's religion, but he had a strong sense of an afterlife, of a God directing in human affairs and lives.

"There's no life to come," Snesia maintained stubbornly, brown eyes flashing. "We have to make the best of this one, Frank." End of discussion, as usual.

6

HIGH WEST

*T*he dusty Volkswagen van with Pennsylvania tags eased to a dust-swirling halt at the end of the access road. Blocking the way ahead was a towering ridge of high peaks that stretched south up into Yellowstone Park and north to the Rocky Mountains.

"This is where the fun starts," announced expedition leader Frank to the five others in the van. There were whoops of enthusiasm all around as they spilled out of the van and began to unpack the hiking and climbing gear.

They had planned this three-week expedition out west for months now. Now they were here. Jack, co-leading the team with Frank, had brought along his girlfriend Sylvia—good company for Snesia. Rounding out the group were Robert and Adrian, young med students with a great interest in the outdoors, but still green in the methods.

"That's Down's Peak up ahead," said Frank, comparing the towering uplift with the map. "We'll head toward it and then follow the mountain ridges all the way along to Gannett Peak. We'll be getting up high in the world by the time we hit that peak."

The others laughed in anticipation and began shouldering packs for the week's trek. Soon they were striding single file through the woodlands hugging the lower mountains.

There was a stirring in the bush ahead of them, and two grandly antlered elk trotted away, heads erect and regal. "Nothing quite like those fellows in Pennsylvania, eh Frank?" commented Jack. Frank nodded at the wonder of the sight.

A little farther on, a half-dozen deer broke cover and dashed away to their left. The two women exclaimed at the smooth, rapid flight of the dainty creatures.

By the time they paused for a break, the climb had steepened considerably, and bushy woodland had given way to the timber stands and rocky outcroppings. Up ahead were vast sheets of last season's snow. In the distance they could see the stark peaks of the Grand Tetons. It was a magnificent scene.

Some hard climbing later, they were on the ridge peak and working their way up and down, toward 13,800-foot Gannett Peak. Frank was in the lead, the others were strung out over quite a distance, and Jack, somewhat impatiently, brought up the rear.

Abruptly the ridge ended at a windblown cornice—an area where wind erosion had formed a drop-off that tucked back under. The top of the cornice was about twenty feet above a super-steep slope perhaps 400 feet high. The entire slope was covered in a thick sheet of wet, slushy snow.

Frank pondered the obstacle for a while, and then decided to rig up a rope on the cornice and repel down to the snow slope with their equipment.

He had the rope attached and was about to lead off with the first pack when Jack caught up with them.

His impatient eyes took in the scene. He saw the women and two young students standing around as Frank went through a classic routine for descending a rock slope. "What *are* you guys doing?" he demanded rather brusquely. And before anyone could answer, he launched himself, pack and all, into the air over the cornice.

He hit the slope with a wet plop and continued rapidly down the wet slide. At the bottom he dug in his heels, stopped, got up, and looked back at his dumbfounded teammates.

Snesia was next, and like sheep over a fence they tumbled over the cornice and down the slope to meet up with Jack. It was actually a lot of fun after the initial heart-stopping leap.

For a few moments they stood around, slapping the snow off their packs and laughing together at the sheer thrill of the descent.

Maybe it was because Jack had so casually leaped past Frank as he cautiously set up a repel. Maybe it was because the leap had actually panicked her. Whatever the reason Snesia took it into her head to angrily deride Frank for the incident. She sat down heavily on a bare rock and announced that she was going no farther. "This is just another ridiculous trip that Frank has manufactured in his head," she burst out. "I am sitting on this rock, and I am not going one more step." Tears of anger and self-pity welled up as she sat there sobbing openly.

Frank and the others didn't quite know what to do. There were a few surreptitious snickers, some self-conscious attempts at humor. Then the five of them walked on to the next rocky area, about 400 feet farther on, and set up for lunch. It took a while, but eventually Snesia stopped crying and very meekly came over and joined the group. They were in the adventure together, and there was no turning back.

Up on the mountaintop the danger seemed strangely distant and benign. It was real, though. It was just masked by the intoxicating thrill of the visual grandeur.

They followed the ridge for several days. Each day the climb was more difficult and the views to the surrounding country more panoramic. Beneath them the mountains almost writhed like giant earthbound reptiles. Somehow it made mere specks of humanity seem more significant by treading lightly down the reptiles' spines.

There was another incident of suspended terror when they crossed a high, exposed scree landslide slope. It was steep. So steep that to fall would guarantee a 1,200-foot tumble to oblivion. The entire surface of the slope was fine, loose scree. It kept slipping from under their feet.

Snesia and Sylvia were numb with fear.

Frank and the others ferried their packs across the slope and the small ledge at the end. But even with the deadweight of a pack, Snesia was shaken with shivering fear.

It took many long minutes to coax the two women across the gap. Their fear was accentuated by the fact that as the somewhat rounded slope fell away before them, its very contour hid the drop below them. The effect was one of sliding across a crumbling bridge suspended in the sky.

Snesia was burning with anger when it was all over. She was angry at being exposed to such danger, angry at her own powerlessness, and, of course, angry at Frank for bringing her to such a spot.

Continuing past the scree slope they found that they were on a vast plateau near the mountaintop. Again they felt lifted bodily to a floating platform in the sky. All around them towered other grand and rocky peaks.

"Fantastic," exalted Robert, swiveling around to catch the panorama in one cinemascopic view. He lost his balance and sat down heavily. "Absolutely fantastic. I've never seen anything like it."

The plateau ended at a glacier that descended perhaps 3,000—4,000 feet.

Again Jack took the initiative. "Let me check this out," he announced, sitting down on the soft snow-ice. He held his ice pick behind him as a brake and then pushed off downhill. The pick left a roostertail of ice as Jack sailed rapidly out of sight down the glacier, vanishing for a moment in a concave section of the fall and reappearing a moment later, moving even faster.

As Jack neared the bottom of the glacier, they could see him dig his heels into the soft ice and ease to a stop. His pick had stabilized him as he slid down the ice, but it took deep heeling with two extra flying tails of ice spray to slow him down.

Frank and the others saw him stop, turn, and wave the go-ahead. His distant antlike figure at the bottom accentuated the fact that it was a long way down. It must be safe, though, and he didn't seem to have encountered any crevasses.

"Let's go," encouraged Frank, with a surreptitious glance at Snesia. She seemed willing enough for the great slide.

It was fast. It was all each could do to control his or her descent with the ice picks. A few seconds into the slide they were whooping and yelling with glee. Great spray trails of ice shot up across the glacier as they descended.

Halfway down, the snow turned a soft pinkish color. Some sort of fungus had taken in the ice, giving it a deep gemlike color. It was an unforgettable experience for all. After stopping at the bottom, they rested for a long time, wet and excited, reliving the experience and reveling in the high excitement.

They continued on down between two towering sentinels of rock. Looking up at the sheer rock walls rising thousands of feet on either side was a reminder of the scale of things in the universe. Puny humans couldn't help but be awed by such massive majesty.

At the end of that and every day that week, they sat around a warming campfire and shared their impressions of the trek. As always on such adventures, the group felt bonded by their shared experiences. Even Snesia warmed to the magic of such moments. It was a happy time for all.

By the weekend they were back down at the minibus.

"Stage two of 'Adventure West' coming up," promised Frank as he drove them up north a few miles to the southern border of Yellowstone Park. The plan was to spend the second week hiking along the high country on the Yellowstone/Grand Teton Park border.

This time the going was a little easier. Snesia made a few remarks about the second week being more pleasant, and no one argued with her. The thrill of danger was missing, but to a group of easterners the almost extravagant beauty of Yellowstone was a constant high. Deer and elk moved in front of them in a constant display of primeval plenty. The first time they startled a feeding grizzly bear and sent him scurrying and huffing for higher ground, there was no sense of danger, only wonder.

By the end of the second week they had grown together as a group. Frank and Snesia were back on good terms—not that there was anything terminal to Snesia's outbursts. "Just be thankful you've got someone like me who will put up with you," Frank joked to Snesia one night; "no one else would." Perhaps he was right. But perhaps they fought because they were so much alike and their love produced not only warmth but sparks that could consume.

Two weeks of hiking had hardened the muscles of even the two novices. They were all fighting fit and ready for another challenging segment to the wild West adventure.

Near the end of the week, Adrian summed it up for them all

when he spotted the distant peaks of the Grand Tetons. They were just breaking camp after the last night of the hike when he saw those rough contours through the trees. "Let's go climb the sky again," he said, and the others felt it was time to return to the heights.

The VW van sputtered the miles away as they headed east to the Big Horn Mountain of Wyoming. "Next stop—Cloud Peak," exulted Frank. It had been a great trip so far, and Cloud Peak, 13,167 feet of rocky challenge, promised even more excitement.

7

AT THE END
OF A ROPE

C loud Peak." It had a rather soft, otherworldly title. In reality, though, it was a tough granite fortress plugged into the dry Wyoming plains. It was high, all right. High and cold. Glaciers gathered around its upper heights, and freezing winds whipped the bare summit. This was the final challenge for the "wild West" group.

It took quite a few hours for the group to hike up from the road to the base of the peak. That climb itself was a challenge. The beauty of the scene was awe inspiring. As they got closer to the peak, it seemed to engulf them and dominate their world.

Jack looked up at the forbidding peak and quickly sized up the situation. He scanned the gigantic chimneylike rock formation on the way up, calculating the best way to approach it. "There's only one obvious way up," he said. "That ridge should take us pretty high up the chimney formation and get us near the top without much trouble." He began gathering the climbing ropes and checking the packs of pitons and other gear. Snesia and Sylvia looked in horror at the wall of granite in front of them. Sylvia shook her head emphatically, and Snesia spoke up quickly. "There is no way we are going with you up that cliff." Her eyes

were flashing, and Frank knew that fear and stubbornness
would prevail this time. He had to answer her, however.

"But, honey, the guidebook says it is only a 5-5 rated climb—
easy for beginners." He tried to sound convincing. While he
thought she could handle the climb, he had his doubts about the
5-5 rating. The book wasn't factoring in that it was clearly an all-
day climb, and that it was ice cold up there even in August. In
fact, a storm had lashed the peak a few days earlier and had
clearly laid down a lot of ice, making the climb even more difficult.

"We'll wait here for you," said Snesia with an air of finality.
Discussion ended.

So the four men began the ascent. Frank had no question
regarding Jack's climbing ability, but he was rather worried
about Robert and Adrian. They were new at that type of climb,
and he would have to watch them very closely.

Jack went first, probing the rocks for the most direct route.
Robert and Adrian followed him, easily at first, then more
cautiously, with a hint of fear in their movements. Frank took up
the rear. He carefully monitored the progress of the two above
him, calling out instructions as they clung to the rope that Jack
periodically attached to the solid granite face with pitons and
wedges.

As they climbed higher the rock face became sharply steeper.
Their progress slowed. Rest stops were more frequent.

"Take a look down there," Jack directed as they paused
against the rock face for yet another session of straining upward.
Frank and the others looked out and over to an almost heart-
stopping scene below them.

There to one side of the final peak was a glacier lake. It held
an immense body of floating ice. With what they feared was a
hint of things to come, violent winds battered the lake and
moved the glacial lump through the waters. They could see
waves on the windswept surface, like ripples on a pond. But
what looked like ripples from so high above were almost
certainly waves a couple of feet high.

Best not to look down for too long, Frank reminded himself,
thinking of the two beginners. "OK, let's keep moving," he called
up to Jack. "We don't want to get caught up here after sundown."

As the climb steepened, Frank began to calculate the risks. At first he rationalized that a fall without a guide rope would probably break a bone or two. Now and then they had to take risks that Frank knew carried greater consequences than a broken bone.

Near the top they came to the chimney formation. It was about forty feet high, solid rock on three sides, open on the other. The roof of the chimney was overhanging rock, while down below there was nothing. Frank heard the two beginners suck in their breath when they saw what had to be done.

Jack went first. Skillfully he pounded in the anchor spikes and wedges to attach the rope. Then he stepped out into the clear space of the chimney. There was nothing below him for about 400 feet. One wrong move, and he would fall cleanly out of the chimney like a free-fall sky diver onto the rocks below.

He reached the top of the chimney at length and paused before the really tricky part. The hood of the chimney hung over the funnel, and he had to climb out and over the lip. Frank and the other two climbers watched him quietly. No time to panic the man.

They heard him give a little self-satisfied cheer up above. "Who's next?" he called down in good spirits.

"You go next, Robert," suggested Frank, basing his choice on nothing other than that Robert was a little older than Adrian.

Up above, Jack anchored the rope and held it steady for Robert. Down below, Frank anchored his end and braced just in case. Jack hadn't mentioned it, but the ice deposited in the chimney by the recent storms added considerably to the risk of the climb.

Robert pulled himself from one anchor point to another, his feet scrambling frantically for a grip. At one point his foot dislodged a large chunk of granite. It fell noiselessly through the chimney and down onto the flaring rock base below. No one else noticed it, and Frank said nothing.

Robert was totally terrorized by his predicament. His muscles shook from adrenalin overdose—he was literally crawling up the chimney.

Up above, Jack was getting impatient. "Come on, Robert," he bullied, "we can't wait all day."

"Give the kid a break," shouted Frank.

"I'm cold, and it's getting late," responded Jack, in no mood to be charitable.

"Don't complain, Jack," Frank coaxed. "You were a beginner once. A little patience is all you need."

Frank almost expected Robert to fall. The prospect only mildly troubled him. He was on a rope, and he and Jack could easily check any fall. Oh, he'd get a few bruises and the scare of his life, but he'd survive.

Time crawled by more slowly, it seemed, than Robert's progress up the chimney. He didn't fall, though, and after forty-five minutes was at the chimney roof. His legs shook alarmingly from nervous exhaustion.

Jack took matters into his own hands as Robert crept up and out. An impatient heave on the rope, and he had Robert at the edge. Another pull with Robert wildly scrambling, and it was over. Once on top, Robert was ecstatic. He slapped Jack on the back and laughed nervously. Jack handed him the anchor rope and then called down to Frank to come up.

Looking up the chimney, Frank suddenly realized just how late it was. The interior was deeply shadowed in the failing light. High above, surrounded by the aura of setting sunlight, he could just see Robert holding the rope firmly and bracing for the pull.

"Here goes," he said to himself, and swung out into the chimney. Almost instantly he realized why Robert had been in such trouble. Cracks and chinks, so necessary for rock climbing, were iced over or smoothed out by thick ice sheets. The difficulty factor was now way above the guidebook's optimistic figure.

Several times as he edged into the crack, his hand slipped on the ice, and his weight pulled against the rope. It was not pleasant. Summoning all his nerve and experience, Frank grappled out over the lip of the chimney roof.

"Easy there, we've got you." It was Jack pulling him up, with Robert maintaining the tension on the rope. Even in the cold, thin air, Frank was aware of perspiration dripping down his forehead.

"Thanks, Robert," huffed Frank, still out of breath from the last effort. He was surprised at how firmly Robert had supported the rope given his shaking muscles of a few minutes earlier.

"Oh, you were safe enough," reassured Robert. "I had the rope base anchored to the rocks." He gestured toward where the rope looped around a boulder.

Frank gasped reflexively. The rock weighed no more than 300 pounds. If he had fallen, the jerk at the end of any fall would have easily pulled the boulder over and down on top of him. He opened his mouth to bawl out the helpful young greenhorn. The words stopped midbreath. Why bother? It was late, and they were in the middle of unfinished business.

"Come on up, Adrian," he called down; "it's your turn."

"I can't do it," Adrian shouted the words up the chimney. He was panicked, and the hollow echo of his words off the rocks underscored his refusal.

Frank was mad and perhaps a little panicked himself. They had taken far too long on the climb already. It was late, and the weather was deteriorating. His response was immediate.

"You grab that rope this instant and get yourself up here, do you hear? We'll have to leave you otherwise." It was an unrealistic threat given seriously. Adrian swung out under Frank's protection and scampered up the chimney. He was a fair enough climber. It had been a loss of nerve, not a lack of skill.

After the chimney the next few segments seemed easy. Jack worked furiously, hammering in supports and coaxing the others up the difficult sections. Then, when it was almost too dark to see the rock face, they made it. Robert let out a whoop of triumph as they tumbled up over the edge to stand on the plateaulike summit. The entire peak was shaped somewhat like an upside-down ice-cream cone—and they were now standing high up on the slightly flattened tip of that cone.

"That was great," Robert gushed in the first pause. "I'll never forget that chimney climb as long as I live. Although for a few minutes back there I thought my life expectation was pretty limited." They all laughed to share the release of tension. It was comforting to laugh about dangers past, but the present danger was real enough.

Up on top, the wind was cutting and surprisingly cold for an August evening. They had come prepared for a summer climb—T-shirts and shorts had seemed just right when they set off.

"It's going to be a cold night, fellows," Jack announced, just to let the others know the obvious. They would have to spend the night on top. Already it was too dark to see much of the rock face below the edge. Their world was limited to the few square yards of the plateau.

"The girls will be worried," voiced Frank.

"Yea, Sylvia will have a few words to say when we get back," concurred Jack.

"But I'm sure they'll wait till tomorrow before they figure we're lost or anything," Frank added. They both regretted having underestimated the climb. It would be a long night.

The four men huddled together on the rocks, keeping low to protect themselves from the ever colder evening wind. It was dark and desperately cold.

Far below on the open plains the lights of towns and small cities winked on like fireflies. "What a sight," exclaimed Robert.

"I've never seen anything quite like it," agreed Frank, spellbound by the sight.

They were high above the plains. The rock pinnacle itself was around 1,400 feet, and in the darkness they seemed to be lightly suspended in magic space. The lights of the distant towns glowed and twinkled all around them. It was possible to make out the glowing pin lights of a city about eighty miles away. And then the atmosphere would change subtly, and the lights vanished. Perhaps it was caused by a diffusion layer in the night air, or perhaps there were wispy clouds moving by with just enough density to block the light. Whatever the cause, the effect was the most wonderful display of light and space. Watching it, Frank was caught up in the magic of imagination. He felt the powerlessness of his humanity and at the same time experienced a surge of reverence for a God who could direct such immensity. There had to be meaning beyond the hustle and everyday business of human concerns. There had to be a higher reality.

The temperature continued to drop. They huddled closer together for warmth. Back to back they sat on the bare rock, their bodies quaking in the cold. Frank gritted his teeth to stop them from chattering together. There was nothing he could do about the freezing air moving through his seat and into his bones.

"I can't take it any longer," Jack announced icily after about twenty minutes of the first huddle. "Let's stand up." So the group stood up, still together for warmth. It eased the problem of cold from the rock, but they were even more exposed to the icy wind.

"My hands are numb," complained Adrian, pounding them together.

"Down again, then," instructed Frank. So they ended the first of many sit-down, stand-up, sit-down cycles. About every twenty minutes the cold rocks forced them to their feet, and then, always, the wind froze them down again.

The moon came out, and its light opened up the details of their discomfort on the summit. "Why don't we climb down in the moonlight?" suggested Frank.

Even in the dim moonlight he saw the positive response on Jack's tired face. "Why not?" he said; "we could be back down before dawn if the moon stays cloud free."

They stood up again and edged toward the drop-off to spy out the descent. Frank looked over the precipice and groaned. "There's no way we can take this thing tonight. The moon's bright up here, but just take a look at the dark rock face." There was just enough moonlight to show the dark immensity of the peak. It looked even tougher in the moonlight. Frank's stomach tightened, and he turned back to huddle again with the others.

Somehow they survived the night. No one slept. They were cold and stiff when the first fingers of dawn stretched out and slanted across the peak. It took a long time for the early morning sun to chase away the shadows and somewhat defrost their perch.

"Man, am I stiff," moaned Frank as he stretched and got up for what seemed like the thousandth time. "Got to get some blood moving," he said, and he circled the narrow peak area as well as he could, waving his arms vigorously. One by one the others followed suit.

"What a night," moaned Adrian. "Let's get out of this place. I couldn't take another night up here."

"Well, at least the going down will be easier," Frank assured him. "It'll pretty much be straight rappelling from here to the base of the rock face—about 1,400 feet, I'd guess."

He coiled up the rope into careful loops, ready for the descent. It was a 165-foot rope, so they would be down in no more than eight or ten rappels.

Jack anchored the rope, and it was over the edge for the first rappel. Frank was amazed at how easily it went. One by one the four of them rappelled down the rope. It was almost fun, even with cold-stiffened muscles. Frank was last man down on the first drop. With arching outward leaps he launched out from the rock face—one hand adjusting the tension of the braking loop around his body and the other guiding him down the main rope as he fell fast. A few leaping slides, and he was down on the next ledge where the others waited.

It took only a moment to flick the rope free of its previous anchor and set it up for the second rappel. It couldn't have gone more smoothly. They'd be down in time for a late breakfast.

Jack led off, moving confidently to the next natural ledge. Robert and Adrian followed, each a little hesitant, but clearly gaining confidence. Both Frank and Jack called out instructions as first Robert, then Adrian moved down the rope.

The second rappel, and Frank made it easily. There was a natural rhythm to the way he slid down, and his leaps off the rocks were undisguised joy. He felt good about the climb. Sure, they'd had a bad night, but then they'd also seen the night magic over the Wyoming plains. He would never forget that almost mystical sight.

At the ledge Frank jerked the rope to dislodge it from above. It didn't budge. He flicked it up a few more times. No luck. It was wedged in the rocks near the anchor point. There was no other way to deal with it. He had to climb up the full length of the rope and pull it out of the crack in the rock.

"Give it another try before you climb up," suggested Jack, impatient as always. Frank worked away at it some more and then jerked at it a few more times with all his weight. It was obvious the knot had wedged in the crack they could just see below the anchor point.

"I'm going back up," announced Frank, angry at having to retrace his recent progress.

"We'll wait," joked Robert. Frank began the long haul up without a smile. He didn't mind the joke, but he was afraid of something no one else seemed aware of. There was a good chance the rope had indeed flipped free of the anchor. If so he was only supported by the knot wedged in the crack. That was OK if the wedge held. But if it should slip free—well, it didn't bear thinking about.

He made it to the top of the rope. It was wedged tightly in the rock, held only by the knot. Relieved at his good fortune, Frank reattached the rope, free of the crack in the rock this time, and rappelled on down to the others.

The next two rappels were very slow. Perhaps Robert and Adrian had thought through the real danger when Frank climbed up the wedged rope. Perhaps they were just tiring more quickly due to their inexperience. Whatever the cause they slowed way down. They seemed to inch their way down the rope, body language signaling a fear to let go and glide.

Jack was getting agitated. He was used to fast, skillful climbs. He hated waiting for beginners. Frank watched Robert coming down and felt more charitable. *Why hassle him?* he thought. *This young fellow is here once in his life. Maybe it's the only time he'll have an experience like this. Why should I deprive him of the joy of the moment?*

"Let me go first this time," snapped Jack impatiently as Robert slid onto the ledge. They attached the rope, and he quickly slid out of sight, appearing at intervals as he bounced out for each rappel down.

Frank knelt down on the ledge to get a better view of Jack's progress. He moved quickly down the face and over a steeply angled ledge, vanishing for a moment in the space beneath it. Then he reappeared near the extremity of the 165-foot rope. At the end of the rope there was a check knot. Jack continued right to the knot. Then he stopped. He couldn't go any farther, and hung there, swaying a little with the rope.

"Why did he do that?" Frank was talking to no one in particular. He was just bothered that Jack had raced ahead so quickly and set up this tricky situation.

"Climb . . . back . . . up . . . the . . . rope," he yelled down to Jack from cupped hands. The words seemed to get lost on the vastness of the rock face.

Jack's options were limited. Because of the overhanging area above him, he was swinging free out from the rocks. He could climb back up the rope—a tedious and tiring exercise as Frank had just experienced. Or he could climb up a bit to the overhang and attach himself to the rock with a chock and just hang there. Then the others would have to come down the rope and hang from the same chock before rappelling down the next 165 feet.

The last alternative was not a pleasant one for anyone, least of all for Jack. It was a scary thing to hang from a rock waiting for others to come and get you off.

It was hard to get the words down to Jack. "What . . . are . . . you . . . going . . . to . . . do?" yelled Frank. Precious seconds went by as he and Jack yelled back and forth.

"I'm . . . going . . . lower." Jack had a plan, but Frank didn't like it. He watched as Jack untied the final check knot to give a few extra feet to the rope.

"There's . . . a . . . ledge . . . below . . . me," Jack called up. By that point he was hanging at the very end of the rope. His eyes were on a fairly wide ledge about five feet beneath him.

"Don't . . . risk . . . it; . . . climb . . . back . . . up," yelled Frank in one last, desperate attempt to get Jack to return.

If he heard, Jack gave no sign. He leapt the few feet to the ledge.

Soundlessly to the three watching from above, Jack hit the ledge, bounced off, and fell free of the rope. He slammed into the rocks, one foot wedging momentarily in a crack. Then the momentum ripped him free, tearing off the shoe and almost severing his foot.

The body fell rapidly out of sight, bouncing between the two rock walls like some limp, boneless mannequin. At the bottom of the rock face the body thumped into a snow gully, bounded its way halfway down, and came to rest at a grotesque angle, the head turned back behind the shoulders.

It took only a few moments—shocking moments—to turn a climbing friend and companion into a mangled heap far below them. Jack was dead, there was no doubt. Now Frank was on the rocks with two rookies, nervous enough to begin with, now shocked at Jack's fall.

Robert and Adrian were frozen in horror. Neither said a word as Jack bounced down into the gully. Their faces were white with fear, eyes wide in terror.

"He's dead," announced Frank brusquely, hiding his own

shock. "There's nothing we can do about it." They looked at him numbly. "I don't want you two guys to go the same way. So get hold of yourselves . . . *right now!*" It was like the military all over again. Frank knew he had to scare them into discipline, or there would be another accident. They were all flushed with fear; the adrenalin rush had left them shaking. Unless they calmed down and followed orders, it would destroy them. They couldn't afford to be shaky on the rope.

Robert and Adrian took his directions. It diverted their fear. "We are going down that rope," Frank announced. "I'll hook into the crack above the projecting area that Jack went past. You come down and hook on with me. Then it'll be easy to run the rope down for the next descent."

They nodded obediently. Frank rappelled down and attached the chock firmly to the hard granite. First Robert, then Adrian moved down and hooked onto the high perch. Frank pulled the rope down and sent Adrian first on the next rappel. They were going to make it!

Seven rappels and six hours later they reached the bottom of the rock pinnacle. They were drained emotionally as well as physically.

"You did well, fellows," complimented Frank. "It should be fairly easy going from here back to camp."

"What about Jack?" wondered Adrian.

"We can't take the body back now," answered Frank. "But we should locate it so a rescue team can find it."

So they headed off down the ice slope. They found what was left of Jack in a twisted heap. In a way it wasn't as shocking as they had feared. The body bore little resemblance to the living being they had known as Jack. It was so battered, broken, and twisted, it seemed only a sad reminder of what had been.

Frank took off the pack and covered the body with snow, marking the spot with a few rocks. "Let's go," he said curtly, anxious to put the grisly scene behind him.

It should have been an easy walk back, but they hadn't counted on the two glaciers between them and camp. One step at a time they stair-stepped their way across the ice, kicking deep toeholds into the slippery surface.

Both glaciers ended in cold alpine lakes. A misstep would have been fatal. The ice dropped off sharply and curved abruptly into the water over a ten-foot vertical fall. In between were numerous ice cliffs and jagged outcroppings. And always as they inched across the ice there was the mental picture of a friend falling onto the rocks, of his body buried beneath the snow, quiet and misshapen. The walk back was dreadful.

Finally they topped a small rise and began the last descent to the camp. Snesia and Sylvia spotted them several hundred yards away. Both girls had a catch of fear as they counted the distant figures. Only three when there should have been four! Was someone hurt, or worse?

For months after that, Snesia would recount the terror she felt when she first saw the three figures. "Someone was missing," she told Frank later. "Instantly I knew it was you. I knew that you had died. My worst fear had come true. I always thought I would die on a climb, not you. But there was the horrible reality of your death staring at me. Three figures—and you were not one of them."

Snesia was mistaken. She and Sylvia walked toward the three men. Coming closer they recognized Frank, Robert, and Adrian. Sylvia paled at the possibility Jack was hurt. "Where's Jack?" she called out.

"Dead," called back Frank in a lifeless voice. "He pulled a Bogle." Both girls were familiar with the climber in Pakistan who died in a similarly impatient move. "His body is back a few miles in a snow gully."

Sylvia burst into tears. She had been close to Jack, and her loss was devastating. Snesia did her best to comfort the poor girl. She looked at Frank and the two others, awkward in the presence of an open grief they shared inwardly. "There's food on the stove," she directed, her own tears beginning to flow. "We've been expecting you for hours."

They needed no further encouragement. Quickly they wolfed down every scrap of the food Snesia had prepared. They hadn't eaten since setting off the day before.

Early the next morning, Frank took Jack's pack and walked down to the ranger station. Jack had been single, a young man of 26, with no wife and no children. But he had parents, and Frank wanted them to take care of his personal effects.

"I've come to report a death in the mountains," Frank told the ranger, "a climbing accident." The ranger's eyes widened. "We've got to get the body out," added Frank.

"Where did this happen?" was the ranger's first question.

"Back up at Cloud Peak," said Frank. "The body is in a snow gully below the rock face."

"I'll get help immediately," said the ranger. He called up the state headquarters and after a rapid round of calls and discussions told Frank that the governor had cleared a national guard helicopter to come get the body.

Several hours later the heavy *thump thump* of helicopter blades signaled its arrival. It was a big military helicopter, manned by four national guardsmen. They looked confident and professional, but Frank had doubts about these weekend warriors. Two of them wore big dark glasses, like Dennis Hopper and Peter Fonda outlaws, and they all had an air of confident nonchalance that bothered Frank.

As the copter settled down, the tall, lanky pilot gave a self-conscious wave to Frank and the ranger. Maybe it was to impress his passengers. The door swung open and out stepped a chubby sheriff's deputy, clutching a walkie-talkie.

"OK, now, where's the body?" he snapped officiously at Frank.

"Hold your horses, Al," checked a voice behind him. It was the sheriff, an older man with the air of someone on a constant campaign trail.

"Don't worry, son," he told Frank; "we'll have your friend's body out of there in no time."

It took a bit of map searching to pinpoint the spot where they could land and recover the body. Frank wasn't impressed by the chopper pilot's knowledge of the terrain.

"We'll stop by your camp and get your two buddies," boomed the sheriff as the helicopter gathered height. "They can help us move the body down to the chopper." His voice was almost drowned out by the accelerating blade noise. It lifted off easily, and as the pilot pushed the joy stick forward, it tilted away in a surprising burst of speed.

With Robert and Adrian aboard they took off once more for the base of Cloud Peak.

"Down there on the ice," yelled Frank as the copter scooted high over the snow gully.

"No way, buddy," yelled the pilot. "We'll set down in a flat area and send you out to bring the body in."

Not too far away there was an area of high pasture. Flat land surrounded by rugged outcroppings and the skirt of mountains. The chopper set down easily.

The deputy sheriff walked back in with Frank, Robert, and Adrian. He wasn't used to the exercise and did a lot of huffing and puffing in between long, breathless sessions on the walkie-talkie.

Back in the snow gully they uncovered Jack's body and placed it in a sleeping bag. They figured it would be easier to carry that way. There wasn't much talking as they struggled back through the snow and along the rocky foothills. The body was amazingly heavy. Heavy and hard.

Nothing seemed to be going smoothly. When they got back, the pilot announced that he was taking the chopper out to refuel. "Don't worry," he said, "we'll be back shortly." Frank had further worries about these weekend warriors. He didn't know what they were up to.

When the helicopter had gone far enough to allow easy talking, Frank turned to Robert and Adrian. "Look," he said, "there's no need for you two to travel back in the chopper. It'll take days to tie up all the details. Why don't you go back to the van and drive back to Philly with the girls? Tell them I'll follow later."

"No way, Frank," answered Robert; "we're in this together."

It didn't seem more than a few minutes till the big chopper was back. It hung noisily for a moment and then settled with its rotors turning slowly.

They hoisted the body aboard onto a stretcher. Robert and Adrian climbed aboard. The guardsman at the door crosswaved his arms to indicate they were too loaded to take more passengers. "We'll be back later," he yelled above the rising beat of the blades.

Frank and the sheriff deputy stood off to one side near a rocky outcropping to observe the takeoff. The chopper faced into the rising ridges of the pass into the mountain, and Frank knew they would have to turn around and go back the way they had come in over the meadow.

He was wrong.

Through the glass he could see the confident smile of the pilot as he gunned the engine to maximum and pulled the chopper up almost vertically, heading toward the pass. He clearly intended to hop up over the pass and then turn back to town. From the moment he lifted off, Frank could tell it wasn't going to work. The chopper shuddered violently and then began to lose altitude.

It happened so quickly the pilot probably didn't realize he was in trouble. One second the chopper was rising slowly in a shadow, the next it fell off to the side in a violent turn. It was obvious the pilot had tried to turn back to the meadow.

The blade struck the rocky wall of the pass. There was a grinding metallic clatter as they disintegrated against the rock. The air was filled with whistling fragments of metal. Without blades the helicopter crumpled onto its side, with the engine still running.

"Get on the walkie-talkie," yelled Frank to the stunned deputy. "Get another chopper in here—fast." He barked the words at the man in his best military style.

"Mayday, mayday. We have a chopper down near Cloud Peak . . ." began the deputy, mouth pressed against the transceiver.

Frank ran ahead to the chopper, an agony of fear tearing at him. His two friends were in there. He saw it lying on a flat, rocky area, its engine roaring like a wild animal. Clouds of steam were blowing off the downed machine, and as he got closer, Frank saw fuel bubbling out of the ruptured tanks.

It's going to blow, he thought, *and my two friends will be incinerated. This trip is jinxed.*

Then he saw them struggling to open the greenhouse window. It broke loose, and they tumbled out like some frantic progeny birthed by the roaring wreck. Frank pulled the last crewman out, and the group rushed back to a safe distance. "Thank God, you're alive," he said with a hurried embrace for each of his two companions. It was nothing short of miraculous that the four national guard crew, the sheriff, and Robert and Adrian were not injured in the fall or burned in the explosion that should have followed.

The deputy came over with news that another chopper was on its way up to get them. It took quite a while, and the waiting group sat and watched the chopper in silence. Eventually all the gas bubbled out of the tanks. Deprived of its life the engine stopped roaring. And it was quiet. There had been no fire, and it was cold.

What next? thought Frank. *That's two bad incidents—what next?* They were picked up by a privately owned chopper. The pilot was used to flying among the ravines and peaks of the Bighorns. He came zipping along around the obstacles, as though it were a trip to the corner store. Frank felt a lot more confident when he saw his style.

There was one last person to rescue from the crashed chopper. Very carefully they moved the sleeping bag–shrouded form across to the smaller chopper.

As the chopper took off for the first of a number of shuttles to get the group out, Frank was full of foreboding. He had his movie camera with him but didn't dare take a sequence of the chopper taking off. He was sure it would jinx the operation. He was not thinking rationally. His fear was paralyzing his judgment.

But in spite of Frank's paranoia they were all shuttled safely to lower ground. The pilot dropped Frank, Robert, and Adrian off about halfway down to the city. They traveled the rest of the way on horseback. That was a story in itself. Neither Robert nor Adrian had ever ridden a horse before. Robert slipped in the saddle and fell under the horse. Adrian lost his grip and bounced off the back of his horse. Everyone had a good laugh. They needed it. The trip had been no laughing matter.

It was the first time Frank had seen someone die on a climb. He had always recognized the dangers—even luxuriated in them. But it was hypothetical before. Now it was real. And he would never quite outlive its shadow.

Robert and Adrian went back to Philadelphia with tales of the exciting expeditions Frank put together. It was the experience of their young lives. Others in the University of Pennsylvania Outing Club murmured that Jack had died because of Frank's unsafe climbing methods.

8

GETTING AWAY
FROM IT ALL

D ean Gannet was furious. "Kelly, you are the most insubordinate medical student I've ever come across." He
slammed the office door shut, strode across to his desk,
sat down heavily in the padded seat, and swung toward Frank.
"You can't just take any day off," he growled, stabbing his finger
accusingly toward the unrepentant student.

"Would you have given me the day off if I had asked?" tested
Frank gamely.

"Why, of course. But you have to ask, and you didn't, Frank."
The medical-school dean was not taking the matter lightly.

Frank didn't like the logic of the situation.

"Look, Dean, I'm not a kid anymore, and this is not a prep
school for young kids. I've been an officer in the army. I've had
six years of work experience as an engineer. I've earned all my
own expenses for medical school." He omitted the G.I. Bill assistance, but in a real sense he had earned that too. He paused for a
breath and continued with mounting indignation. "I'm a responsible person. There is no way I am going to duck out during an
emergency or when someone is counting on me."

"But you didn't ask." Melvin Gannet leaned forward in his

chair, brows bristled up and a big blood vessel bulging on his forehead. "You have no respect for authority."

"How did I do it wrong?" Frank asked. "I took yesterday off. The day before, I came to you and said, 'I'll be taking tomorrow off.' You knew I'd be away."

The vein on Gannet's forehead pulsated rapidly. "That's just it. You have it the wrong way around. You just can't tell me you are taking a day off—even though it might be granted easily enough. You still have to *ask* for it."

It was Frank's turn to boil in reply. "What an arrogant way to deal with the situation! I am not a child. I am an adult; I am a human being, and you can treat me with the dignity I deserve."

Dean Gannet whirled around to the file and jerked the drawer open. He ran his finger along the index tabs to K, then pulled out the "Kelly, Frank" file. It flopped open on the desk, and the dean glared at it angrily.

"Luckily for you, Kelly, your grades are good. Somehow you've fooled your professors into thinking you want to learn. But—" and he looked up suddenly, eyes heavy with dislike. "Don't think you're getting away with this. I'm going to include a report on this insubordination in your academic file." He wasn't bluffing. Frank knew that at once. Gannet wound a sheet of paper into· the typewriter and began his denunciation of a problem student.

"That will be all, Kelly," he said curtly.

Frank went out the door quickly, turning as he pulled the door shut for one last look at Gannet stabbing the keyboard in his rage.

They were both mad. Frank felt the same rush of rebellion he remembered from arguing with his father about a career choice. It was the same challenge of authority that poisoned his military service. And in a very real way his outdoor expeditions were a challenge, an upraised fist, against providence and conformity. It was no accident that his climbing methods were unorthodox and his equipment generally handmade and nonstandard. Frank was opposed to any attempt to mold him into conformity.

"That vindictive old man will give me trouble," he told Snesia that night after supper as they discussed the incident. Snesia was supportive as she invariably was when he needed affirmation.

"Don't worry, Frank," she encouraged, her brown eyes managing the subtle mixture of fire and sensitivity he loved. "You will do well as a doctor, I know it. Your grades are good, and there's nothing that mean assistant dean can do to you." She snuggled closer to him on the small settee positioned diagonally in the apartment living room.

"Oh, he'll make things difficult, all right," sighed Frank, his arm around her. "Before the day was over, I heard that he had bad-mouthed me on two of the school staff committees . . . tried to maintain that I am deficient—in what way, he can't really say, though."

"So forget him," instructed Snesia, tired after her day at the hospital and confident Frank would do well in spite of the dean. She believed in him.

Frank didn't feel like studying that night, so they relaxed together with the TV, fresh popcorn, and each other. Their marriage had come a long way since those moonbeam ideals of college days, but if anything they were more in love than at first. It was wonderful to enjoy a quiet time together.

"You know some of our hiking buddies wouldn't believe this," joked Frank.

"What do you mean?" asked Snesia.

"This pleasant domesticity. On expeditions we are pretty rough and tumble. I'll wake up in the morning and bawl out orders at you, and you'll snap back, and we'll snarl at each other a bit."

Snesia nodded. Sometimes they were at each other's throats. "Yes, and I'll call you a silly so-and-so for getting us into another crazy mess." Frank smiled a little ruefully at that remembrance.

"I love you, Snesia," he repeated. And it was the only answer to put the talk of camping arguments in true perspective. They loved each other, no doubt about it in Frank's mind.

He was probably no different from all the other happily married men in the world, he guessed. Take any of them aside and ask how they would rate their relationship with their wife, and most of them would say, "Oh, I'm madly in love with her." It wouldn't matter that they just had a shouting match with their wife that morning. They would look at the whole picture and see nothing but love. That's how Frank felt about Snesia. He loved that wild, independent girl who gave him real trouble.

He couldn't imagine any limit to his affection for Snesia. Oh, sure, every mountain had its peak, some point of ultimate attainment. But Frank knew enough about love and life to expect no such finality to love. He and Snesia had experienced great adventures together, they had loved, fought, studied, and cried together. They had faced tragedy together in many ways. To such a growing love, Frank reasoned, there could be no end, no final attainment.

The conflict with Dean Gannet proved to be enduring. He lost no opportunity in bad-mouthing Frank to faculty members and other visiting doctors. Frank tried to shrug it off, but as graduation time came closer he began to think Gannet might have the upper hand.

"Made your perfect match yet?" joked Stephen Childres one morning as they passed in the hallway between lab sessions. "I linked up with my second choice yesterday. I was hoping for that hospital in Boston, but my name came up for the top hospital in Cincinnati." No wonder he was happy. "I think the dean put in a good word for me," he twinkled mischievously. Smart aleck!

"No, nothing yet," glummed Frank to the initial question. "Maybe I need that good word!"

Stephen swept on by to his class, leaving Frank to muse on the situation. Coming up to graduation all the med students watched the postings closely. The idea was to line up a hospital in a prestigious location, a place with a strong staff and lots of potential for advancement. Most of the graduates were already paired up with assignments by now. Frank was one of the few left hanging.

It wasn't for lack of trying. Frank found out to his dismay that the computer had failed to match him up to any of the places he requested. He'd requested spots at quite a few western hospitals. Maybe that was the problem. There were perhaps 250 applicants for no more than ten positions in those areas. It had him worried plenty.

Like others who came up dry on the initial matchup, Frank got on the WATS line and called direct to a few likely spots. Nothing like applying in person, even if it was by phone.

Invariably, after the initial chitchat and a few signs of

progress, he was asked the same question. "Mind if I talk with
the dean about it, Frank? Just a backup check, you know."

He got a quick reading on what he could expect on that count.
The first time he hooked the dean on the line was enough. Right
away he began to badmouth Frank, downplay his ability, his attitude—any negative to spoil Frank's chances. "You don't want
that guy;" he said in essence, "he's a real loser."

Frank felt doubly betrayed. Whatever the dean felt personally,
it was his job to do the best possible for his students. There was
no way he was authorized to downplay a student like that.

By the time he got around to calling the VA hospital in Huntington, West Virginia, Frank was pretty desperate. He was running out of hospitals to call and running out of time. Tentatively
he dialed the number and asked for the medical director.

"This is Cecil Anderson," boomed the voice at the other end.
"What can I do for you, son?"

Quickly Frank filled him in on who he was, his good grades,
and, of course, his need to find a residency to intern.

"Am I glad you called," laughed the director in a reassuring
way. "I need residents real bad. You're on, boy."

"Do you want me to transfer you to the dean?" asked Frank,
knowing he had to test the opportunity.

"No need, Frank," boomed the big voice pleasantly. "I need
doctors so bad I'll take anyone. We need you."

Frank took it as a joke. It never occurred to him that Cecil
was dead serious. He had a lot to learn. The beginning of that
process was the discovery that Dean Gannet had originally come
to the medical school from that same VA hospital at Huntington.

Still, it was a posting. And in the country too. He had become
consumed with a need to escape the hassles of big-city life. This
job in Huntington was his ticket out.

Snesia didn't share his enthusiasm for leaving Philadelphia.
The two of them had quite an argument when Frank told her of
the upcoming move.

"Huntington . . . West Virginia!" she exploded. A quick look at
the map confirmed her worst fears. Huntington was a little town,
by itself in the corner of West Virginia, next to Ohio and Kentucky. "It's way out in the sticks. I don't want to go to a backward
area like that. Why didn't you line up a hospital here or near

some decent city?" She was almost hysterical.

"There is no way I am going to stay in Philadelphia," asserted
Frank, ready to outshout her to a decision. "In my opinion, big
cities are the cesspools of civilization. I'm sick of seeing the corruption and decay here. I'm nauseated by the rat race, the traffic
snarls, and the metropolitan superficiality. I've got to get out.
We've got to get out, Snesia."

In the face of Frank's deep-seated hatred for city life, Snesia
backed off from her first line of reasoning. She switched to
darker objections.

"I'll be lost in Huntington, Frank," she almost wailed. "A place
like that will be culturally depressed. It won't have the social life
I like here. What about nightclubs, nice restaurants, entertain-
ment? They don't have that kind of life in Huntington, do they?"

Obviously Frank didn't know. He hoped not, but they'd both
have to wait and see. For the moment he pulled Snesia close to
soothe her panic and his own uncertainty. It was a big move.

Very unwillingly, Snesia gave notice at the VA hospital where
she worked as a pharmacist. Her co-workers shared her indignation at Frank for wanting to move away. It was only natural.
Snesia had endeared herself to many at the hospital. She was
tactful, although not at all tolerant of incompetence. She was
warm, loving, and friendly, with a smile for everyone.

That smile became very subdued after she left Philadelphia.
Frank had turned her world upside down.

They left for West Virginia in July 1981. The drive down to
Huntington confirmed Snesia's worst fears. Mile by mile the
scenery became more rural. Close to Huntington they passed
through small towns distinguished by rotting clapboard and
hayseed types outside the country stores.

Frank saw it a little differently. This was the real America.
This was a chance to reach out and touch real people. He was
looking forward to the internship; beyond that, there would be a
rewarding country practice, genteel living, and perhaps a
cheaper model Mercedes. He imagined the gracious country
home they would eventually build—and of course, the children.
Their careers had come first until now, but soon they would have
to think about starting a family.

Cecil Anderson, the medical director at the Huntington VA

hospital, seemed just as genial in person as on the phone. "Welcome to Huntington," he boomed when they walked into his office. "You'll love working here, Frank. We are a pretty informal outfit, and we'll do our best to make things pleasant." He put his arms around Frank and Snesia as he ushered them out for an orientation tour around the complex. "It's so great to have you young people here," he repeated. Snesia wasn't smiling. Her doubts about Huntington had already become reality. She hated it.

Frank found his new responsibilities fascinating. He quickly found that the West Virginians resented any suggestion that the area was backward. Perhaps in Huntington itself there was some evidence to counter the myth, but out in the more rural areas up on the mountain valleys, Frank found the reality of life for West Virginians was closer to the cliché.

He spent a lot of his time doing rounds in the outlying clinics. Up in the hills he came across areas isolated by poor, unsealed roads. He saw communities almost cut off from civilization, places where the people rarely, if ever, left their own little valleys. He saw families enfeebled by inbreeding. He met people—pioneer types—living in log cabins, fiercely independent, and suspicious of modern medicine.

One day a very pregnant mountain woman limped into the clinic. She was nine months pregnant and ready to deliver. Normally she wouldn't have bothered with a hospital for something as common as childbirth. She came in to the clinic needing treatment for her injured hands and feet.

The woman laughed as she told staff members the cause of her injuries, but the injuries were real enough. It turned out that her father and her husband had fought over who owned her.

Her husband had originally stolen her from out front of her house and claimed her as his bride. Actually up in the hill country, that was an accepted way to get a wife. Much later a dispute developed between her husband and her father. The older man demanded his daughter back. Her husband refused. Before long the situation degenerated into a physical battle for possession. The woman's husband had hold of her legs, and her father had an equally firm grasp on her arms. By the end of the twisting, pulling, and bending, the poor woman was in bad shape. She answered their argument for possession by leaving and walking down to the clinic. Amazingly she thought the whole incident hilarious.

It wasn't long before another barefoot hill lady walked down to the hospital for emergency treatment. Someone had taken a golf club to her head and lacerated her scalp pretty badly. The fix-up required ninety-six stitches.

What really impressed the staff was the woman's hygiene. This hill lady was probably around eighty years of age, and all indications were that she had never taken a bath in her life. Her bare feet were black with dirt. From there up her skin was lighter and lighter shades of gray to her chest. From there on up she became dark gray again. They made her take a bath.

There were real needs in Huntington, and for the first time Frank realized the role of medicine in helping ease suffering and ignorance. Sure, there were the usual tensions among staff at the hospital, but overall he was content, at home, and more sure of himself and his role.

At Hahneman Medical School in Philadelphia he had played the part of a rebel—an independent rebel. It was no wonder that he antagonized the staid Dr. Gannet. Less acceptable had been the bad report on his medical rotation. Perhaps because of the influence of Dr. Gannet, the doctor in charge of rating the medical students on their medical rotation, a Dr. Kamler from the University of Vermont, harshly criticized Frank's performance.

"The young man is dangerous," he told the dean in his evaluation. "He'll kill patients if we don't check him in." Frank fumed about that evaluation for a long time. In Frank's mind, Dr. Kamler himself was the one killing patients through ineptitude.

In Huntington, Frank had sweet vindication. As an intern at the VA hospital his performance was regularly rated by supervising doctors. Dr. Ed Robinson gave Frank an excellent rating on his internal medical rotation—a five-star report. This Dr. Robinson had previously been senior resident at the University of Vermont. He had, in fact, been Dr. Kamler's boss. Kamler may have failed Frank, but his boss had rated Frank highly.

For the first time in years, Frank saw sunshine ahead. His dreams were coming true. Every morning he woke up to the smell of country air; he saw flowers along the way. This was living!

Snesia, in contrast, was deeply depressed. There was nothing she liked about Huntington. Life there was unbearable for her.

Every evening Frank's sunny mood was tested by her tirades against life among the hillbillies.

"I'm sick of this culturally deprived hellhole," she began, with what was already a familiar routine.

"It's really not that bad, honey," soothed Frank, still on a high from good ratings at the hospital.

"It's worse, Frank. There's nothing for me to do here. I might as well be dead. My future is empty." She was depressed and aware of it enough to use it against Frank. "You dragged me away from my friends in Philadelphia. You dragged me away from a great job where I was appreciated. And why? Just because you want to be in some hick area. Just because you want to smell the roses. Big deal. But what about me, you selfish oaf?"

It wasn't really Snesia's style to be so derogatory to Frank, but her style had changed radically in the few weeks since they arrived at Huntington. She had little to do but nurse her frustrations. Frank looked at the coffee table in the lounge—there was quite a stack of library books. At least she was keeping busy by reading. However, he didn't like the emphasis of the titles he could see from across the room. For starters there was one called *The Independent Woman,* and several others on self-assertiveness. They were the last books Snesia needed right now.

She eased up on the tirade against Frank for bringing her to Huntington and started a different line of attack.

"Maybe we're not right for each other, Frank," she began coolly. "Maybe we need to separate for a while. Experience other things. Get to know ourselves. Maybe—"

Frank was horrified. He had no intention of letting Snesia just drift away.

"Don't be silly, honey," he interjected. "We belong together. We are married, remember! We love each other."

"Yes, but what if we separated for a few years? If our love is strong, it will survive. I'm sick of sitting here in West Virginia letting the world pass me by. I've got to be free, Frank," and she ended her plea by collapsing on the couch in tears.

Frank was stunned. He knew Snesia loved him. Sure they fought. Who didn't? But from the beginning theirs had been a passionate relationship. They enjoyed each other's company. They complemented each other in so many ways.

Her words echoed in Frank's ears: "I want to leave you . . . I don't love you." They were words he couldn't reconcile with the Snesia he knew and loved. They had to be words and ideas born out of her absolute dejection at life in Huntington. He knew from experience Snesia loved him. Others had told him the same story. On more than one occasion, Snesia's co-workers had come to Frank and remarked on her obvious love for him. "She's crazy about you," they told him. "You are a lucky man to have a wife so loyal," they said. Others told him that in conversations with them, Snesia had expressed her deep and unconditional love for him. He needed to remember those testimonials now. He had to fight off her present depression and clear the way for love again.

Snesia was sobbing violently. Her trim figure appeared almost wasted by the way she sprawled limply on the couch. Her usually-smiling brown eyes were puffy and half-hidden by her hair.

Frank looked past her to the front room of the apartment. It was their exercise and equipment room. Leaning up against the wall were their well-used kayaks. One whole wall was covered in mountaineering gear, snowshoes, and skis. Additionally, they had thousands of dollars worth of specialized equipment used for such activities as vertical caving. These things represented their most challenging shared experiences.

He moved over to Snesia and put his arm around her, soothing her hair back from her face.

"I know just what you need, Snesia," he began sympathetically. "You need to get away from Huntington for a while." He had her attention instantly. "Just the other day I received a note from the Pittsburg Explorers Club announcing a three-week trek in Peru. I think you should go."

"Without you?" Snesia was clearly interested.

"Why not, honey? I trust you. I only want the best for you." They kissed gently as a seal to the deal.

A little later the phone rang. It was Snesia's parents. They were none too keen on the move to Huntington either, seeing only the possibility of fewer visits from a favorite daughter and spoiled son-in-law.

Snesia chatted cheerily with them for quite a while. Obviously she was in a better frame of mind and changed to English for a word to Frank.

"Dad wants to talk to you," she said. "He's in a very protective mood. Try to reassure him."

"Hello, Milan," he began; "good to hear from you."

"What is this about your letting Snesiana go on a trip by herself?" It was a father speaking, not merely a friend.

"No trouble, Milan," Frank reassured. "It's a large, professional expedition. Snesia wants to go, and I think it will do her good."

"Her mother and I worry," persisted Milan. "You young people play games with danger. Think of your parents, and then worry." Frank couldn't think of an immediate answer, and Milan continued. "We have entrusted our daughter to you, Frank. Take care of her. We are fearful something will happen to you or to Snesia on one of your adventures."

"I promise she'll be all right," said Frank.

Milan's voice dropped a little of the initial tenseness. "When are you both coming back to Michigan to visit us?" he asked, not very hopefully.

"Not for a while yet, I'm afraid," answered Frank a little guiltily. "But we think of you often. Give my love to Radmila."

"Well, goodbye, Frank. Take care of her."

"Goodbye."

They always worried about Snesia.

"Let's plan the details of my trip now," bubbled Snesia. "I can't wait to leave."

She had the time of her life on that trip to Peru. Frank had no worries about her safety. The Explorers Club prided itself on its level of expertise. And on an expedition all the members ate and slept together as a community. They would take care of Snesia. He had no fear of her compromising herself with any male team member. He knew his Snesia. She would handle any situation. She loved him.

Snesia came back from Peru with the old sparkle in her eye. She was superbly fit after three weeks trekking in the Andes, and Frank guessed she was ready for more.

"I've arranged another trip for you," he announced. "A friend of mine named Don is leading a group out west to climb in the Rockies."

"How long this time?" was her main question.

"Another three weeks."

"Thank you, Frank. Remember, I love you."

Again the trip was a success. Snesia came back with a new maturity, a new self-confidence.

"I'm glad I sent you on those trips," said Frank. "I've got some good news. There's an opening at the VA hospital for a pharmacist. The job is yours if you want it."

Snesia threw her arms around Frank's neck. "We'll be working together. How wonderful!"

The job signaled the end of Snesia's depression. She was a lady with a need to be involved, and the pharmacist job at the hospital gave her that opportunity. Soon she was doing far more than the typical pharmacist. She put together fact sheets for the drug reps to give to the doctors. She began to advise the doctors on how to use the different drugs. In fact, it wasn't too long before she was doing the morning rounds with the doctors, giving expert, ongoing advice on drug treatments.

Frank thought it was marvelous that she was able to go on rounds with him in the morning. He took special pride in knowing that this competent pharmacist was his wife. He took special satisfaction in noting that she quickly gained the respect and admiration of most of the staff.

Oh, at first there were a few awkward scenes. "Dr. Norich was very short with me today," she complained to Frank.

"Oh. Anything the matter?"

"I don't think he appreciated the note I sent him saying he was doing the wrong thing in prescribing those two drugs at once."

Frank laughed. "You've got to treat doctors gently," he said. "You're dealing with big babies here. When you write notes like that, make the doctor think it is his idea. Agree with him. Try saying, 'It is wonderful of you to realize that we shouldn't administer these two drugs. I totally agree with your decision. It shows great sensitivity to the patient's delicate situation.' Remember to soothe their egos."

Snesia had no more problems with doctors. One after the other they came to Frank and commented favorably on her expertise.

Frank was ecstatic over her ready acceptance at the hospital. Maybe she'll even get to like Huntington, he thought wistfully.

"Don wants me to go with him and another friend on an ice-climbing trip to Huntington Ravine in New Hampshire." Snesia dropped the news almost casually—too casually—and Frank immediately read much more into the situation.

"He's got a thing for you, hasn't he?" said Frank.

"Maybe. It doesn't matter. I'm only interested in learning how to climb." Snesia dismissed his fears quickly with her casual statement of fact.

"Just the same," pursued Frank in the jealous-husband mode, "keep an eye on that guy. You're my wife, you know."

"Thanks for caring, Frank."

"And remember, safety first when you're climbing."

"Don't worry about me," she reassured. "You're the one who needs watching. I think you'd be dead or crippled by now if it weren't for my holding you back."

She had a point.

"Just keep your distance from Don," he laughed.

Frank thought about Snesia every moment she was away. He was proud of her and worried about her indecision at the same time.

While Frank was assisting in the operating room one day, the conversation turned to Snesia.

"We haven't seen your wife much lately, Frank," said one of the young nurses.

"Do you know where she is now?" asked Frank in reply.

"No. I guess she's at home watching the soaps," was the expected guess.

"Wrong," announced Frank triumphantly, reaching for the suture tray. "She's probably halfway up an ice cliff in Huntington Ravine, New Hampshire."

He knew Snesia was an exceptional woman. The nurses showed by their wide eyes that they agreed.

The end of that year Frank and Snesia joined a group of about forty-five from the Pittsburg Explorers Club on a trip up to the

Mount Tremblant ski area near Montreal. They drove their van up to Pittsburg and joined the group on the long drive up to Montreal. They expected it to be a great outing, as Mount Tremblant had the reputation of offering the best cross-country skiing in North America.

Frank was particularly keen on cross-country skiing—the traditional way. His skis and the set he bought for Snesia were the Norwegian style—handmade wooden boards in the old style. He wasn't too impressed by all the high-tech skis and equipment most people used. Again, he was doing it his way.

The skiing at Mount Tremblant was all Frank had hoped for. Mile after undulating mile of lightly wooded trail areas. Nothing to disturb the peace but the gentle laughter of friends out on an expedition together and the constant shushing swish of ski against snow.

At night they sat around the warm, crackling fires in the lodge and swapped tall tales and advice on skiing.

Snesia got to talking with several of the women on the outing and soon picked up some interesting skiing tips.

"Frank told me these wooden skis give a better, more natural feel," she explained the first time one of them questioned her equipment.

"Oh, Snesia, you're too trusting," remarked the woman. "Frank has some pretty far-out ideas on equipment, doesn't he? Take my advice and try the latest laminated fiberglass skis. They're so much better."

"And the new quick-release bindings are the only way to go," added one of the other girls.

"Go high-tech all the way, girl," advised the third woman. "You can get rid of those wooden poles. Get the new lightweight ones."

They all seemed to know what they were talking about. Maybe Frank wasn't quite with it on skiing equipment. Snesia thought of Frank tackling some of the higher slopes on his handmade skis and home-brewed equipment. He obviously enjoyed the challenge of the tricky setup. But maybe he didn't know any better. She knew he took risks. She knew of his reputation for being unsafe. Maybe it was true. She remembered how the University of Pennsylvania Outdoor Club used to list Frank's expeditions. At the bottom of all the weekend outings they would write "Frank Kelly's trip to the sun. Guaranteed to be different."

"Yes," she said at length, "I will try the new equipment this winter. Perhaps Frank isn't quite up on what's best for cross-country skiing."

Overall, Snesia was a big hit with the women in the group. They were impressed with her open, forthright manner. They envied her trim, fit physique and the smart way she dressed. She had an approach with people that was disarming—a truly winning personality.

Near the end of their stay at Tremblant, a group of women stopped Frank to comment on his wife.

"We really admire your wife," said one.

"She is our idea of the ideal woman," said another.

"You must be very proud of your wife," added a third before Frank could answer.

"Your wife is the woman that every American woman aspires to be," continued the first by way of summing up their opinion of her. Frank was flattered. His little Snow White had come a long way from a shy teenager, fresh out of Yugoslavia and unable to speak English.

Both Snesia and Frank left Mount Tremblant with happy memories. It had been a wonderful time. It was a reminder to both of them that the love of outdoor activities was a common bond.

On the way back their conversation came around again to the dangers of mountaineering and other wild adventures.

"I know I've done some pretty crazy, outlandish, headstrong, things, Snesia," agreed Frank. "There's a really good chance I'll die on one of them. But that's the risk I'm willing to take. The adventures are worth that risk."

"You are right," agreed Snesia, remembering the first pact they made years earlier at the beginning of their mountaineering adventures. "It's a risk we have to live with. I explained it to my parents once. They worry so much, you know." Frank nodded; he knew. "I told them not to worry. That I could take care of myself. Still, if something were to happen to me, I told them, then cry all you want for three months. Then after that, go back out and enjoy life. I won't know anything more, and I wouldn't want them to grieve too much."

"But it won't happen," said Frank, knowing in his heart that he would die first.

"Don't grieve for me if I die, Frank," implored Snesia. "I've enjoyed life. Whatever happens will be the way it's going to be, and we can't change it. And then if I die, that's the end of it."

"No heaven, no tomorrow to hope for?" tested Frank, always bothered by Snesia's defiant belief that there was no larger spiritual dimension to life beyond a creator who started it all.

"This is all there is," she maintained. "If we die, that's it."

"Let's live life to the full, then," encouraged Frank. Maybe one day Snesia would look to the stars for help. Perhaps it was her curse to be so independent. In the meantime he would look out for her.

9

ALONE

F rank turned his back on the hiking hut and moved out along the high trail. Late-season snow crackled faintly beneath his heavy boots. The day had been crisp and sunny. Now, afternoon shadows reached low and long over the ridges. He quickened his stride. He had to reach the car and drive to Hardee's restaurant before nightfall.

Calm and white topped, the Allegheny Mountains softly dominated the scene. They were not yet quite awake from their winter sleep. Their quiet alpine peace stood in sharp contrast to the turmoil of Frank's thoughts.

It had begun a few weeks earlier with a call from their friends in Philadelphia. Snesia answered the phone and was soon an enthusiastic part of their plans.

"You're driving down to West Virgina for Valentine's weekend," she repeated excitedly. "Sure, Frank and I would love to join you." A quiet aside to Frank, "Wouldn't we, Frank?" He nodded. "It sounds perfect. We'll meet you at Seneca Rocks for a weekend of hiking and rock climbing. We'll be looking forward to it. Goodbye, Don."

Frank was immediately defensive at the mention of Don. "What's Don got planned?" he quizzed, suspicious at the start.

"Forget Don," said Snesia; "you've no cause to worry."

Frank kept right on worrying.

They met the group from Pennsylvania at Dolly Sods, about thirteen miles from Seneca Rocks. It was rather early in the season for rock climbing and easy hiking, but the weather had been unseasonably mild. Bright sunlight denied the late-winter reality of the mid-February weekend.

The group of adventurers gathered at the local Hardee's restaurant to go over the plans for the different activities. It turned out that most of them had decided to trek up on the high trails and rough it at night in the various hikers' huts along the way.

"While you guys head for the hills, we'll be tackling Seneca Rocks," announced Don with a quick look at Frank. "I'm taking Snesia and Ed to the rocks for an intensive training session." Frank recognized the intent of this announcement at once. "I'd like to come, too, Don," he said.

Don flushed as he answered, "Snesia needs the time away from you to concentrate on her rock-climbing skills. Don't crowd her, Frank. I'll teach her the right techniques."

His answer only heightened Frank's suspicions. He moved with Snesia to a more distant table before putting his case to her.

"What is this with Don? Are you in on this, Snesia?"

She laughed good-naturedly. "I told you not to worry. Sure, I knew that Don didn't want you along. It's too bad, but he just doesn't want you along. He says you are unsafe. He told me you were a risk to any expedition."

Frank almost gagged at the idea he couldn't accompany his own wife because another man claimed he was dangerous.

"That's not the real reason, is it?"

Snesia shrugged her shoulders.

"The real reason is, he's after you. He is saying, I don't want you to come because I like Snesia myself and I want her to be my wife."

"That may be the case," acknowledged Snesia, "but it doesn't matter. I want to learn rock-climbing skills, and Don is very competent and a good teacher. I'm not going to let jealousy get in the way of that."

Frank calmed down a bit. "I only want the best for you, honey," he said. "Just don't let Don talk you into anything other than rock climbing."

"You're too jealous," concluded Snesia.

"Promise me one thing," pursued Frank. "That you'll meet me back here Sunday night. Let's celebrate Valentine's Day together before we drive back home."

"Oh, I don't know about that, Frank," said Snesia. "Don already suggested we stay an extra day or two. I can easily take the bus back to Huntington."

Her answer sent a thrill of terror through Frank. "I'll be here Sunday night," he repeated as they moved to rejoin the others. "Don't forget, Sunday night at Hardee's."

"Don't count on it, Frank," she replied. Frank drove off with the main group heading for the mountain trails. Snesia joined Don and Ed, a raw beginner, for several days of rock climbing. Their plan was to practice technique at a nearby rock quarry and then head off to Seneca Rocks on Sunday for a shot at the real thing.

Dangerous. He says I'm dangerous. He wants my wife. Why am I up here? I shouldn't be here, I should be with Snesia. All weekend Frank turned himself inside out with worry over the situation.

For perhaps the first time ever, Frank was untouched by the raw glory of the high-mountain scenery. On Sunday the sun rose rapidly to a beautiful golden warmth. It was unseasonably warm. Frank noticed only the cold, ice-covered rocks in the shadows. Clear skies did nothing but show him better the curling clouds on the horizon. He was miserable and apprehensive. He walked the trails in an uncanny fog. Why was he so far away from Snesia?

His hiking companions sensed his discomfort. They knew only that he was somehow jealous of his wife off climbing with Don. They could never comprehend the complex anxieties he was experiencing.

Frank said goodbye to them at the hut and turned toward the downhill trail. He must hurry. Snesia would be waiting for him at Hardee's. Maybe when he joined her he would cease vibrating with anxiety. Maybe then he would lose the feeling that his world was teetering on its axis.

Once in the car, he expected the dizzy disorientation to end. It didn't. Each curve in the tree-lined roadway made it surge up again. Not too far now. He'd soon be there.

Along the road he spotted a fruit-and-curiosity stall. There was no fruit this time of the year. Plenty of old treasures and a few bottles of preserves, though. Maybe he should buy a little gift for Snesia—a Valentines' gift. Next to the preserves he spotted neat rows of honey jars. "I'll have that jug of honey," he announced to the storekeeper, who came over with questioning eyes.

"Four dollars, son," the man announced as he placed the jar in a paper bag. Frank moved his hand around in one pocket, then the other. The total haul came to just over four dollars. He paid for the jar and drove on.

Finally, the Hardee's restaurant. It looked rather empty and deserted before the evening rush. The jug of honey under one arm, he bounded up the stairs, through the door, and looked around. No Snesia. Perhaps he was a little early. Frank moved to a corner and sidled behind one of the bench tables.

"Are you Frank Kelly?" The waitress asked the question more by way of confirmation. Frank was clearly a hiker in from the cold, and the young girl had been waiting for him.

"Yes, I am," answered Frank in surprise.

"I have a note for you," she said, holding out a folded piece of red paper. "The lady left it a day or two ago and said you would be here late Sunday afternoon."

"Thank you," said Frank, his voice almost cracking with apprehension. What could the note mean?

"Dear Frank," he read, "I told you not to worry. I'll meet you at the restaurant later tonight. Snesia."

He knew Snesia would come through. He shouldn't have even imagined that she was anything less than faithful. They would have a wonderful evening and a special day driving back to Huntington together. Frank even looked forward to hearing Snesia tell the details of her rock-climbing exploits.

* * * * *

Earlier that day the three rock climbers unstowed their gear and looked Seneca Rocks over once more. Both Snesia and Don had climbed the rocks a number of times before. It was a first for Ed.

Snesia pulled on the special gloves she used for rock climbing.

They were cut off at the fingers to give her better grip on the rocks. Frank regularly scoffed at the theory behind these gloves. "Sure," he would say whenever Snesia defended them, "they'll keep your palms warm. It's your fingers you should be warming, though. You might as well wear paper gloves."

If Snesia remembered Frank's opinion of the gloves, it was only against the opinion of Don. "Frank is a dangerous climber," he kept repeating. "I wouldn't want him on one of my climbs."

With the others, Snesia laced on her heavy climbing boots. Each put on light climbing packs for the more specialized tools and fittings they would need for rock climbing. Don came over and checked both Ed and Snesia's packs, pulling a little on the clips of Ed's pack. "Looks good," he approved. "Let's go."

The first part of the climb was basic stuff—"chicken-easy" climbing, according to Don as he outlined the climb plan. "No need for special climbing precautions till we hit the steeper stuff," he told them.

The air may have been warmed by the wash of sunlight, but the rocks were cold, icy cold. In the shadowy cracks, the rocks were cold and covered with ice sheets in spots. All three of the climbers were bothered at first by the numbing effect on their fingers—Snesia especially.

Don moved on ahead, pointing the way up an easy crack in the face. It sloped up toward the steepest rocks. "Follow me up through the crack," he instructed his charges. "Once up there we'll regroup and start using the ropes." The route he took looked easy enough: gently sloping, loose rocks, and plenty of spots to grip in tight with fist and fingers.

Ed followed Don, moving very awkwardly, as he was still very green at the whole rock-climbing business. Somehow he made it up OK, in spite of a few slips when the ice nearly got the better of him.

Snesia came last. She wasn't overly concerned at the difficulty of the first part of the climb. Don said it was a "chicken-easy" climb—no need to worry. They'd use the ropes later. Her 150-foot rope was coiled up on top of her pack. It would come in handy later. If only the rocks weren't so cold. As her fingers numbed up, Snesia found it increasingly difficult to feel and maintain her grip.

Then, as she grappled for a wedge grip about halfway up the large crack, her fingers slipped. Her weight shifted slightly, causing her to lean back a little. In an instant the dead weight of the pack was pulling her back and over.

Don and Ed heard Snesia cry out in panic. As they watched, in a frozen moment she fell away from the incline, thumping heavily against a protruding tree. She was flailing the air for a grip, too panic-stricken to grasp the tree for support. She fell free and plunged headfirst onto the rocks about 150 feet below. There was no movement.

Don quickly slipped down the slope and checked Snesia's injuries. There was no sign she was alive. The back of her head was smashed and a mass of oozing blood.

"Go get an ambulance . . . *quickly!*" yelled Don to a frightened Ed. Ed ran off while Don began a desperate hour-long effort to revive Snesia with CPR. He was still trying when the ambulance came. Back at the hospital they continued the attempt to revive her. There was no sign of life.

* * * * *

Waiting at Hardee's, Frank was getting a little impatient. He expected Snesia well before this. Where was she? Looking out the window he saw Don pull his truck into the parking lot. He was alone.

Frank watched him slowly walk up the stairs, open the door, and look fearfully around inside the restaurant. He spotted Frank and walked over with an ashen expression on his face.

Frank read it all in an instant. "Is she dead?" was his first question.

"Yes," answered Don. "There's been a terrible accident. Snesia is dead." Then the words tumbled out as he told the basic details of the accident, of Snesia's fall, of her death. He was still in shock.

Frank's world had just come to an end. Soon he would fall into the deepest shock possible. But his immediate reaction was, take care of business. It was Cloud Peak in Wyoming all over again. There were other people to take care of, details to be seen to. An inner voice seemed to be saying "Be cool. Do what you have to do right now. Call her parents. Go and see the body. Keep calm."

There was a telephone at the front of the restaurant. Frank went to it and dialed the number he knew so well. Milan answered the phone. "Hello, Frank," he replied, his voice showing simple joy at hearing so unexpectedly from a favorite son-in-law. At the sound of his voice, Frank almost broke. What could he say to the man who loved Snesia as much as Frank himself.

"Snesiana *Umerla*," Frank said in Yugoslavian. "Snesia is dead."

There was a cry on the other end of the phone, a cry like a wounded, dying animal. And instantly the others in the house cried out in agony. Frank heard their grief over the phone. It was inconsolable. He was never to see Milan smile again. That day, the joy of life left him. It was the most difficult phone call Frank ever made. He was the bearer of death to a family he loved. Their tears flowed freely; his were imprisoned with the deep sobs that were still to convulse him.

He put the receiver down. "Where is the body?" he asked Don. He knew he had to identify Snesia. As a doctor he had to see her injuries. He had to know how she died.

"She's in a nearby nursing home," said Don. "Come, I'll take you there." Numbly Frank followed him out of Hardee's. It was the last time he ever set foot in a Hardee's restaurant.

At the nursing home he looked at the still figure of the wife he had known and loved for thirteen years. She was only thirty-three.

He saw the signs of the fall. Her intestines had been ruptured in the fall against the tree. She had fallen against the rock, smashing the back of her head. It was a mass of multiple fractures. It was obvious she had died swiftly—probably dead before she hit the ground.

With the eyes of a doctor he analyzed Snesia's injuries. With the heart of a bereaved husband he yearned to somehow bring her back, to rekindle the flame that had so warmed his life.

It was impossible to stay long. He turned away as a tide of memories swept over him.

"Where do you want the body taken?" It was the voice of a helpful policeman.

"She's going home," said Frank. "I want her flown to South Lyon, Michigan."

Then he drove back down to Huntington.

Word of the tragedy had already gotten around by the time he arrived back home. There was a stack of groceries waiting for him there—practical gifts from kind friends who understood the situation. He would never forget their kindness. In spite of it, though, Huntington no longer seemed like home. It was an alien place, not even fit for memories.

Frank turned the key in the ignition, started the car, and steered back toward South Lyon.

Somewhere along the highway he caught up with his grief.

It was almost inconceivable that Snesia was gone. He was the one who seemed to court death. It was Snesia who held him back from the edge. He expected to die before he was forty. He would have died a dozen times, but for Snesia—now she was dead.

Mile after numbing mile he thought on his loss, and the grief deepened.

Why had God allowed this? Snesia didn't deserve to die. She was the safe one. It was someone else's stupidity that had killed her; false confidence. And Frank wasn't there because they said he was unsafe. Why, God, why?

Maybe, Frank told himself in his grief, I'd understand if someone had mugged Snesia at night. Beaten her to a pulp. That was one of the realities of life. A risk we all take. But to die so unnecessarily, in an incident that would never have occurred if he'd been there as he intended. Not fair, God.

"How could you do this to me, God?" Frank raged between bitter tears. It was a charge he was to cry out many times in the weeks ahead. He questioned a God who had given him nearly the perfect life on earth—a life with someone in whom he could trust and believe. All around him he saw marriages dissolving into complacency and worse, while his was growing and thriving and becoming more wonderful by the day.

He read and reread the note Snesia had left him at the restaurant. In spite of a jealous rival she remained faithful. She never intended to leave him.

Her love was real. They had shared so much together. He felt so close to her at times that it was as if he could reach out and touch her soul, hold it in his hands. Now it had slipped through his fingers and was gone—perhaps forever.

Ahead of him on the road to South Lyon, Frank saw nothing but sorrow and loss. His destination was the casket and a hole in the ground. And a grieving family.

"Why didn't you take me instead, God?" He flung the questions at the empty sky. "Why did you have to take Snesia back now?"

He remembered Snesia's own opinion of an afterlife. "What we have now is all there is," was her adamant belief. She wasn't troubled by hopes of another life. If Snesia is destined to go to hell, Frank reasoned, then that is where I want to be. I want to share her fate, whatever it might be.

Why . . . why . . . why hadn't he been there? The endless agony of might-have-beens crowded in on his grieving mind.

Seneca Rocks, where they had climbed together many times before. Seneca Rocks, guarded by stone sentinels of Indian folklore. Those rocks, those sentinels, should have witnessed more than the lone fall of a snow maiden. Those braves in the legend died for love. He, too, would have gladly flung himself off the cliff after her. There would have been no hesitation. He should have been there. "You cheated me, God. I shouldn't be alive," he cried in agony of remorse.

They were waiting for him at South Lyon. Friends from the Pittsburgh Explorers Club were there with long faces and sad hearts. Milan and Radmila held him close as they welcomed Frank home, but there were no smiles.

Everyone said nice things. The Pittsburgh friends remembered the outgoing young woman of ski trail and mountain campouts. An aggressive young woman pursuing her goals in life. A natural leader. Snesia's parents spoke haltingly of their beloved daughter. She was their special pride—a child with accomplishments these simple people from the old world wondered at. The priest intoned heaven's blessings as he sent Snesia's earthly remains to a final resting place. He also said nice things—comfortless to a husband all too aware of her dismissal of any hereafter. Nobody smiled.

And after the ceremony, after the earth, Frank looked at the flower-covered mound and wept. Snesia was shut away from him forever.

He stayed with her parents only a short time after the ceremony. It was too sad. They looked at him, and he knew their

eyes saw a departed daughter. He knew they blamed him somehow for encouraging Snesia to such dangerous outdoor exploits,
for not being there to protect her.

Milan went out of his way to play gracious host to the guests
who came for the funeral. He showed interest in their conversation, asked about their welfare, their concerns. Then when the
Pittsburgh friends left he spent his energies making Frank feel
welcome—a son. His concern for others was magnificent. Frank
couldn't stand it. Every time his eyes met Milan's, they touched
unbearable loss. Frank read the anguish. He realized that he
was a living reminder of a father's loss.

He said goodbye to the family. There were a few tears and
brave words. And he left on the road back to Huntington. He
would never forget them. He would never forget the heartbroken
father. The man who never smiled again. The man who retreated
into quiet mourning.

Frank returned to emptiness. He returned to a sleepwalking
existence. Huntington was a town of strangers—he only lived
there. He was not interested in socializing, barely interested in
continuing his medical career.

"Snap out of it, Frank," urged Efrim Cohen one day, convinced
Frank was grieving unnecessarily. Efrim was a young associate
of Frank's in family practice. "Snesia is dead," he continued.
"You must face the reality of it. Maybe it would do you good to go
out with someone. Get to know other people. Time to start living,
Frank."

"Don't bother me," resisted Frank. "I don't need any help. Besides I don't intend to involve myself with someone else . . . *ever!*"

"Oh, come on," teased Efrim, hoping to cajole Frank back to
reality. "You don't mean that. Snesia was not the only girl in the
world. You can't hate women now, just because of your painful
loss."

"She was everything to me," said Frank. "I put all I had into
my life with Snesia. I invested everything in that one person."

"She's dead, Frank, you have to face it," insisted Efrim. "There
are other people waiting for your friendship—perhaps love," he
added.

"Snesia took all I had, Efrim," lamented Frank. "I haven't cul-
tivated any other friendships. She was my friend. We did every-

thing together. I even estranged my relatives because Snesia and I were always off on trips together—no time to visit them."

Efrim was running out of suggestions.

"Maybe a child from Snesia would have left me a reason for living. I would have dedicated my life to that child. Snesia was my family here on earth, and now she is gone, and I'm alone."

Efrim had no answers.

For quite a while Frank luxuriated in his grief. Then it struck him that it was introspective and actually selfish. Snesia was dead. She was gone. His grieving did not concern her at all. So he spoke to others less about his trauma. He went through the motions of living, of practicing medicine. In his heart he still cherished the memory of Snesia and a determination to move on in search of peace.

10

ESCAPE
TO INDECISION

"Why are you doing this?" Salim was suspicious. There had to be a trick.

"I'm selling off all the bits and pieces I don't need, that's all," explained Frank. Salim, a colleague at the VA hospital, still needed convincing.

"Your van, it is not so old. I know it is valuable."

"It's worth $200 to me, that's all," said Frank. "Are you interested?"

Salim's eyes widened. "I'll take it," he gasped. "I will not call it a purchase. It is a gift. You are giving it to me. Thank you."

Sure, the van was worth more. Maybe ten times the selling price. It was of little concern to Frank. He was getting rid of it all. Everything had to go. All the reminders of life with Snesia, the daily echoes of those happy years together. He intended to sell everything, and then leave.

Salim reached into a back pocket and pulled out his checkbook. Hastily he scribbled in the amount. He was in a hurry, just in case Frank developed second thoughts.

Frank reached for the check, and as he did so he saw Salim's gaze land on the beautiful gold watch on his wrist. He remem-

107

bered now that Salim once remarked that he admired the watch and wanted one just like it. Frank grasped the spandex band and pulled the watch off his wrist. "You like this watch?" he commented matter-of-factly. "It's yours. Take it as a gift; no charge. I don't particularly need it." Salim was almost incoherent with gratitude.

The director stopped Frank in the hallway one day that summer. He'd heard of the clearance sale and read quite a bit into it. "Well, hi, Frank," he boomed, as genial as ever. "Not long now, eh? Internship about over . . . any plans to stay on at the hospital? Or do you intend to set up a family practice in the area?"

"No, sir, to both ideas," said Frank. "I'm out of here in a few weeks."

"Where to?" the obvious question.

"Anywhere, just to get away. I'm tired of the hassles, the hypocrisy of society." Frank hadn't really intended to say anything like that; it was part of his inner rationale to get away.

"You'll get over your wife's death eventually," soothed the director.

"I'm not sure it's her death at all," continued Frank, pushing on in the same way he had shocked his military commander. "I really believe that society stinks, that this world is sick. You beat yourself to death to get an education, to become a doctor. For what? Just a lot of petty, selfish people looking out for themselves. The medical system exists more to line the pockets of the doctors than to heal people."

The director almost staggered at the outburst. "I hope you find what you're looking for, Frank," he said hastily and moved on down the hallway.

Actually, Frank wasn't bitter. Worn out from the battle with himself and his aspirations would better characterize his situation. Back in college he'd used forestry and the outdoor life as a way to avoid the unpleasant aspects of a hard world. In his view society was unbearable—the filth of the cities, the raucous noise of automobiles, the crowded downtown area—he hated it. But he especially hated the hypocrisy, the artificiality, and the greed of the world around him.

As soon as possible Frank intended to put his pack on his back and head for the nearest trail into the woods and escape to contentment.

There were so many things to dispose of. The obvious things like vans and watches went early. That left him with a houseful of personal effects—reminders of Snesia.

He threw open the closet full of Snesia's clothes. It was the strangest feeling. He remembered her form in some of those clothes. Imagination supplied her presence. The moment brought home the bitter reality of his loss. Never again would those clothes fit and cover their owner.

Almost as a ritual, Frank washed the clothes before disposing of them. The washing machine churned and ground and sloshed its way through a lifetime of washing.

It was not enough to wash away the memory. The clothes Snesia wore the day she died had not yet been washed. Frank threw them in the overloaded washer and moved elsewhere in the house to escape the memory. Much later he returned to find the machine broken. It had stopped and plugged up. He opened the cover to check out the problem. The machine was full of blood—blood-red water from Snesia's clothes.

Almost a year after Snesia's death, Frank left Huntington. He hardly knew what was ahead for him. But, of course, he hardly cared.

He drove away from the house he shared with Snesia for almost a year. There was no looking back. Behind the old VW diesel he pulled a trailer filled with his only possessions. There were no photo albums, no boxes of letters, no treasured items of furniture. They were all gone. He packed the trailer with all the outdoor equipment, climbing gear, skis, camping gear, a down jacket, hiking boots, and a sleeping bag. The road seemed to naturally turn toward Seneca Rocks, so he went that way.

That first night he eased the car and trailer into a familiar campground not far from Seneca Rocks. Frank and Snesia had often camped there together. Perhaps Frank stopped that night to see if Snesia was still there. Perhaps it was just coincidence.

It was cold outside that February night. Frank slept fitfully in his down sleeping bag. The cold did not trouble him.

Next morning he looked out on the white, sleeted fields and mountains. Yes, why not go for a cross-country ski before moving on? He unpacked the smooth handmade skis and bound them to his boots. A firm push on the poles, and he was off, gliding away into his wild world.

Unfortunately the snow cover was thin. Far too thin for good skiing. The skis grated and scratched across the frozen ground, but at least he was moving.

Quite some distance from the campground, Frank came across an open field. The clearly defined ridges across the field identified it as part of a farm. In spring the snow-covered furrows would yield yet another crop. For now they were just another obstacle.

Snap! The left ski hit a frozen furrow and broke in half. "What bad luck," Frank muttered under his breath. "I'm virtually crippled with only one ski."

Somehow he struggled back across the field and back down the way he had come. Near the campground he hit a steep slope. *Well, here goes,* he told himself, feeling the almost forgotten thrill of the wild challenge. He slalomed down the hill on precarious balance.

At the campground again he packed his few items of equipment back on the trailer. The taste of the outdoors was invigorating. Frank knew that was where he belonged. It made even more of his baggage unnecessary. He rummaged around in the box of clothes in the trailer. A formal suit—ridiculous symbol of conventional society! Quickly he hung it on a lower branch of a nearby tree. It hung there, arms flapping idly as he drove away. The suit was sure to present a mystery to later campers; to Frank the symbol was clear. It had to stay.

Back in Michigan, Frank called in to see Snesia's parents. They were as kind and loving as ever. He was hugged and kissed and fussed over. But there were no real smiles, and his presence seemed a cruel reminder. He couldn't stand the thought of hurting them anymore. It was time to move on.

One last visit to the grave. He placed a red and a white rose on the winter-white mound. There would be no forgetting. He would see to it that his snow maiden had those same red and white roses every Valentine's Day.

Route 80 led out of Chicago and west to the high country Frank yearned for. He had a plan and a reason for dragging a trailerful of outdoor equipment and supplies across the continent.

Across the border of Wyoming he detoured north to Casper. Ahead lay familiar territory: the stark peaks of the Bighorn Mountains.

In town Frank stopped at a local Kmart. He bought a 32-gallon garbage can and several packs of thick plastic bags. Just what he needed for his plan.

Along the road out of Casper, he spotted a distinctive rock formation. It was a lonely spot. Perfect. Frank turned the VW off the road and clanked over dry potholes to the base of the rock.

No one around; good. Quickly he unpacked a shovel and began digging a deep pit beneath the overhanging rock. It was hard work, and he raised a few blisters before the hole looked deep enough.

Time for the garbage can and plastic bags. Time also to unload some of the other things on the trailer. Frank checked them over carefully: a stack of paperback books, jars of honey, canned and dried food, skis, ropes, hiking boots, crampons, ice axes, climbing shocks, and an assortment of other outdoor gear. Carefully Frank double wrapped each item in plastic before packing it in the garbage can. Finally he sealed the lid on the can and lifted it into the hole. Filling in the hole was much easier, and soon only the circle of fresh earth over the spot gave anything away.

Frank smoothed it over and stood back. Great! No one would ever stumble upon it or ever guess what lay beneath the ground. The entire package was hidden, waterproof, and deep enough to be bearproof. Step one to the plan had gone well. There were six others to go. He dusted off his hands and repacked the shovel. It might be a long time till he returned, but however long, the cache would be waiting. A bumpy ride back to the main road, and Frank pointed the car toward Route 80 again and the Pacific Crest Trail.

Frank knew what he was doing. He saw this trip as a prelude to dropping out of society. He intended to become a wanderer and live the outdoor life. He planned to lay down caches of food and equipment in at least seven locations.

By the time he reached San Francisco, the trailer was almost empty. Its contents lay buried beneath rock formations, near high lakes, and along pine trails. The caches stretched from Yosemite, California, to Biggs, Oregon.

San Francisco was not the site for one of those caches. That summer he had flown to San Francisco to attend a family-practice convention at the Marconi Center. He was still under the immediate shock of Snesia's death. A relative in the area felt he needed to socialize a bit, focus his attention on the living, not the dead. They introduced Frank to Chris Chan, a well-educated Chinese-American woman almost exactly the same age as Snesia. Chris had been sympathetic, and they got along well. Frank reasoned that he might forget Snesia more quickly if he spent time with Chris. She invited him to come back and visit, and the invitation made a lot of sense to the new wanderer.

When he knocked on her door, Frank had no special plan in mind. He could as easily have said Hello, stayed the afternoon, and headed back to the snowcapped peaks, or stayed on as he did.

"Come in, Frank," welcomed Chris when she answered the door. "I'm so glad to see you. I've missed you." She faltered on the last part of the welcome and gasped for breath, coughing desperately.

"What is the matter, Chris?" asked Frank, concerned at her condition.

"Oh, nothing," she said at length when the attack subsided. "It's just my asthma. It comes on bad sometimes."

"I had no idea," said Frank. "You had no trouble when I was here last."

"I was on medication," Chris answered with an explanation that should have raised suspicions at once.

"We'll have to take good care of you, then," determined Frank protectively. Perhaps he was attracted subconsciously to the fact that Chris was a trained chemist or to her exotic foreign manner, or maybe it was just that the idea of taking care of her gave him a function in life. Whatever the reason, he decided to stay for a while.

Frank may have temporarily forgotten his determination to roam the backwoods, but he never forgot Snesia. He was still deeply hurt by her death and emotionally dislocated. On the one level he moved in with Chris. It was matter of fact and almost without emotion. Chris was pleasant, and she needed him. On the more emotional level he was conscious every moment of his loss.

Chris continued to have bad bouts of asthma. Eventually Frank noticed a definite pattern. Chris used the attacks to manipulate people, especially Frank. He looked at her medicines and with a doctor's judgment determined that the medicines did indeed work. Chris had the ability to block out their effect in order to prolong an attack and manipulate people. Once he understood that, Frank had less trouble relating to Chris. He and Chris had many good times together. They seemed compatible, and time passed by pleasantly.

"How would you like to go on a trip to Europe?" Frank asked Chris one day as they talked about places to visit.

"That would be wonderful. I've never been outside the U.S.," she responded with great enthusiasm. "When do we go?"

"Let's go as soon as possible," he said. "The tickets are less expensive at this time of the year, and we won't be bothered by the summer crowds of tourists. We can travel all over Europe on a Eurail pass. You'll love it."

"What countries will we visit? Let's plan it all now," said Chris enthusiastically, going for the world map she kept in the bookcase. "I had in mind England, France, Norway, Yugoslavia . . ." Frank began. He was halted in midsentence when Chris doubled over with an extremely bad attack of asthma.

"Let's give Yugoslavia a miss," she gasped.

"Why?" said Frank a bit peeved and not too convinced of her attack. "I want to go to Snesia's hometown in Yugoslavia. The culture of that country has always fascinated me."

Chris gasped more desperately. "No, you cannot. I won't let you. Let her die, Frank. I want you to forget Snesia." Her outburst surprised him.

"I can almost sense her presence around you, Frank," she gasped. "I'm frightened that you'll slip deeper under her spell. You mustn't go to Yugoslavia. I forbid it." More gasping for air.

Perhaps she is right, Frank mused. Many times he caught himself gazing off into space, almost expecting Snesia to materialize in front of his eyes. He could sense her presence. Rationally he knew that it was impossible for her to reappear.

Under the shock of grief he was conditioned to hope for something supernatural.

Chris's outburst made him realize briefly how susceptible he was in his present state of mind. In spite of himself he felt Snesia's spirit hovering around, and he had imagined that eventually he would find her again. The feeling refused to leave, no matter how logically he looked at the situation. But the more he looked for Snesia, the more he tried to recapture her lost spirit, the more disappointed he became. There was nothing.

Chris was right. It might be better if he kept away from Yugoslavia. "Maybe I'll go there on another trip," he announced by way of dismissing the subject. Chris smiled and breathed a little more easily.

"Let's do it this way," he continued. "I'll fly on ahead and do a little advanced trekking on my own in Norway—I've always dreamed of hiking along the Hardinger Plateau in southern Norway." The real reason for the suggestion was a return of the empty restlessness that first caused him to load up the trailer and head west. Perhaps Chris recognized it too.

"If you like," she assented easily. "I'll meet you wherever you say."

"I'll meet you in London at the end of the year," said Frank. "We can set the exact date a little later. I'll be in touch."

"And Norway?" Chris showed signs of another asthma attack.

"I'll be off as soon as I buy the ticket," said Frank adventurously. Maybe Norway would erase the pain he still felt. He needed another challenge to occupy his mind.

11

ON MY OWN AGAIN

C hris waved excitedly to Frank over the customs barrier. She paused just long enough to retrieve her stamped passport and then ran toward him, arms outstretched in greeting. They embraced happily for a moment, and then it was all talking.

"I'm here, Frank. It's so exciting," Chris gushed, looking around as though she still couldn't believe it.

"Wonderful." He beamed. "I missed you."

"Did you have a good time in Norway?" Chris asked. There had been little communication from Frank since he left three months earlier. Just a few scribbled postcards.

"I was lost most of the time." Frank smiled cryptically. "But I had a great time. The scenery is wild and awesome."

Chris jiggled up and down with the suppressed excitement of the trip. "Where do we go now, Frank? There's so much to see, I don't know where we should start."

"How about at the train station?" he laughed. "Here, let me help you get that pack off your back."

"What an adventure," bubbled Chris. "I'm even looking forward to sleeping on the train."

"It's called Europe on the cheap," said Frank.

The next few weeks quickly became a blur of railroad tracks, borders, stately castles, wonderful museums, and cramped nights on the train.

Winter in Europe is never the best time of the year. Because of the nasty weather, particularly in northern Europe, there were very few tourists.

"I'd still like to go to Yugoslavia," Frank said one day on the train heading south toward Italy.

Chris blanched visibly. "We settled that three months ago," she said firmly. "I don't want to argue again."

"But—" began Frank.

"I don't want to talk about it, ever," she said finally with a slight cough.

They both enjoyed Italy. Walking most places, they saw a rural side to the country missed by most tourists. Now and then they struck up halting conversations with Italian peasants and found the people open and gracious.

As the train carried them across Italy, stopping at various towns, they encountered numerous cathedrals, chapels, and monasteries. The church was evident everywhere. Frank watched the people in the churches as they lined up in pious rows to make confession. He saw the pilgrims place tapers before carved saints. He knew the system of worship it all represented was badly flawed. Neal Isabelle had long ago brought that realization home. Frank was no longer attracted to the dogmas of Catholicism, but the simple faith of the peasants moved him. It was something he lacked, something he needed. Somehow, someday, he might find it.

In Rome they wandered the ancient streets, as all tourists do.

Frank and Chris listened solemnly as the Italian guide took them through the dark catacombs. "Christians lived, worshiped and died here during the years of persecution," the man intoned. *Was it really worth it?* Frank wondered. It must have required a strong commitment to faith to live that way.

Together they toured Saint Peter's and the Vatican City. Chris was having the time of her life. Eagerly she soaked up the knowledge and culture of an old world she only knew from books. Frank saw it all through different eyes. He enjoyed it, too, but every artifact, every statue spoke to his quest for peace and meaning.

"So this is the famous creation scene," marveled Chris inside the Sistine Chapel, craning her neck back in order to see the painting more clearly. "What a work of art!" Frank saw it too. He saw the life-giving finger of God, but saw it as attached to a distant deity who stood by while an innocent woman fell to her death.

The train carried them back again to colder climes.

In Paris they both marveled at the art treasures in the Louvre. Frank and Chris enjoyed each other's company for many shared reasons. A very important common point was their interest in art and architecture, the classical heritage of golden ages. They had fun times together. But, when all was said and done, Frank realized at one point, he and Chris were actually worlds apart in their view of life.

Atop the Eiffel Tower one night, they gazed out at the frosty winter sparkle of that City of Lights. "Beautiful," murmured Chris, reaching for Frank's hand. It was by his side. His gaze was on the lights, his thoughts years away.

"Are you enjoying our trip, Frank?" she asked, voicing for the first time an uncertainty that first took grip during the debate over Yugoslavia.

"Of course," he reassured.

"Sometimes you are poor company, Frank." This was more than a simple exchange. "I think you are still dreaming about Snesia."

"Of course not."

"Or maybe you just want to be by yourself again?"

"Whatever made you think that?"

"I don't think you care for me at all."

"Don't care for you!"

"I see the faraway look in your eyes all the time. You want to leave me and move on, don't you?" Chris began to cough and gasp for air.

"You're wrong, Chris," said Frank, turning her around so he could unzip her pack and take out the asthma medication. "Why, in San Francisco I pretty much lived just to make you happy. At times I felt like your personal physician."

More coughs and gasping. The discussion didn't go any farther. Chris began to fear that Frank would indeed leave. She had
premonitions, and Frank couldn't shake them. It is always hard
to be persuasive when you think otherwise. Almost against his
will, he *was* becoming restless.

Cold weather dogged them all the way across France. In Germany the real cold was deep within Frank. So many things there
conjured up his time in the military. It wasn't necessary to visit
Oftersheim. Signs of the U.S. military presence were easy to spot
in the country—a halftrack by the side of a freeway, a
camouflaged position in a grainfield, or a familiar uniform on
city streets. Painful memories.

And curiously those memories brought back thoughts of
Snesia. She suffered through his years of military service with
him. She, his newly wedded wife of those not so distant years,
was part of those memories.

Chris kept up the pressure in their discussions. "You don't
love me." "I love you." "I don't love you." "You want to leave."
"Don't leave." "Well, go, then!"

Frank and Chris argued their relationship apart. They
caught the ferry across the channel to England, gazing bleakly
at each other the whole time. Chris was certain Frank intended to leave.

There was one last argument in London. Hot words were exchanged. "That's it," gasped Chris in an induced fit of asthma
that Frank had long since ignored as an emotional ploy. "I'm
leaving. Go where you like. You'll have to do without me. I'm
flying back to San Francisco."

Frank went with Chris to the airport. He helped her check her
pack and then sat in the departure area till they heard the
departure call.

"Goodbye, Chris," he said with a formal hug.

"Goodbye, Frank." And that was that.

He walked outside and waited at the curb for a red London
double-decker bus. It didn't really matter where the bus went.
He was wandering again.

The bus route terminated on the southern outskirts of London. Frank shouldered his pack and ambled off into the neatly
manicured countryside. Time would tell where his wanderings

took him. He had plenty of time. Two weeks till his flight left for Chicago and a lifetime beyond that.

Dusk comes early in the English winter. By evening Frank was barely out of the suburbs. He pitched his tent in a small field by the edge of a busy highway. The usual English drizzle was mercifully absent. But it was bitterly cold out in the field. He lay in the tent that night listening to the cars roaring past from one direction and then from the other. Busy people with things to do, places to go. Eventually, the traffic sounds faded, and he drifted off to sleep.

12

THE BROTHERHOOD
OF PAIN

Chicago is a cold place in March. Those infamous winds make early spring especially chilly. No time for outdoor living. The neat little hiking tent in the backyard of an upper–middle class suburban home shouldn't have been there. Neighbors who spotted it shook their heads. Too early. Young boys in the area often camped out, but only in the summers! What was going on at the Kellys'?

Frank unzipped the tent flap and squeezed through the opening to a tinkling shower of ice strands. He stood up stiffly and stretched before standing back to inspect the tent. Yes, it had been a cold night -20° F. Perfect to test out his hand-stuffed down sleeping bag. And the bag passed with a cozy A rating. He took special pride in his equipment. It was more than pride and satisfaction at a job well done, though. The handmade sleeping bag and parka might save his life some night.

"How did the test go last night?" asked his brother Johnathon a little later over a warm breakfast in the kitchen. Two years younger than Frank, Johnathon was a forensic psychiatrist in the Chicago area.

"Perfect," responded Frank. "Everything worked just fine.

Warm as toast," he commented with somewhat of a cliché as he picked up a slice of the real thing and reached for the butter.

Johnathon pushed the butter plate toward him. "So I guess that means you'll be heading off again?"

"Yes. You and Ellen have been very patient with me . . ." Ellen turned from frying eggs on the griddle and waved that comment away. He was family. ". . . but I'm anxious to head up north."

"And on a bicycle, of all things," interjected Ellen.

"Sure," answered Frank, "it didn't cost much—only $120—no more than a bus ticket. And it'll get me to Minnesota just fine."

"I almost envy you," said Johnathon.

"But not quite," added Frank with a smile.

"No. I'm afraid you're still running, Frank. Just the same I wish you well. Have a great time, and play it safe."

Soon Frank was on his way. The bicycle rode easily beneath his weight and the weight of his pack and other equipment. He was on the open road to adventure.

Actually, Frank had a well-thought-out plan of attack. The bike would take him across Illinois to the Mississippi River. From there he intended to cycle up north, following the river through Wisconsin and across to Minnesota. His goal in Minnesota was the township of Ely, up in the far northeast part of the state and right in the middle of the boundary waters canoe area.

For a week Frank pedaled lightly across the countryside. He stopped along the way to read historical markers and any other man-made or natural feature that caught his eye. The weather was still crisp, yet everything around him resonated with the resurgent energy of spring.

One night he pitched his tent in an abandoned farmyard along the Wisconsin side of the Mississippi. The evening air already hummed with insect and animal sounds. Waterfowl along the river cackled and called excitedly till well after sundown. The pause of winter was clearly over.

Early the next morning Frank awoke to a whistling sound overhead. Amazed, he watched the elaborate mating ritual of a dove-sized jacksnipe. The male bird flew rapidly up into the air, higher and higher, until it was a mere wheeling speck. Then as he strained to keep the bird in sight, it suddenly plummeted in

tight circles, whistling loudly. About two feet from the ground
the male pulled up abruptly and flashed its brilliant plumage for
the female.

Ely is the northernmost town in Minnesota before the boundary waters area. It is a land of lakes and untouched wilderness.
Beyond Ely hundreds of lakes dot the landscape all the way to
the Canadian border and join into an almost unbroken waterway—the old *voyageurs'* route for French trappers. Frank intended to obtain a canoe and paddle that route for a year or
more.

Ely had long since become a jumping-off point for all sorts of
adventurers and tourists. It abounded with wild outdoorsmen
like Frank. For a few days he lingered there making acquaintances, exchanging tales with some of them. In their company he
was less inclined to question his own motives in fleeing civilization.

He met fascinating people with plans of their own. A man
named Will Stieger was busy preparing for an expedition to the
Arctic. With the friendship born of common interest, Will and
Frank discussed the details of such a trip. Frank himself toyed
with the idea of heading up through the waterway all the way to
the Arctic. Will was determined in his plans, and sometime later
Frank learned that he made it all the way to the North Pole.

It took a little haggling to convince the canoe dealer. Eventually the two of them settled on a price. For $220 Frank became
the owner of a fine secondhand canoe, complete with paddle, carrying rack, and life jacket. He left the bicycle in storage with the
canoe dealer and paddled smoothly out onto the lake. Ahead lay
a maze of waterways, wooded islands, and solitude.

The first few days were an outdoorsman's dream come true.
Moose browsed in waterweed along quiet shores, raising dripping jaws to gaze almost absently at the canoe drifting past.
Only the ripples raised by their browsing disturbed the mirrored
tranquility. Waterfowl winged gently overhead in gathering
flocks. Lake beaver nosed across the water, vanishing with a
plop whenever the canoe came too close. It seemed like Eden
revisited.

Life quickly developed its own unhurried routine. Gliding
along in the late afternoon stillness, Frank would scan the shore

for a likely campsite. *There—that rocky headland looks ideal.*
Gently increase the paddle pressure on the other side to swing in
a smooth arc into the shore. The canoe scrapes up on the shore
and pauses in an easy rocking motion. Frank grasps the sides of
the canoe, crawls forward and out onto the rock-strewn lake
shore. Perfect! He pulls the canoe onto dry land and unpacks his
gear.

The campsite is only about six inches above the lake level—a
lovely low spot with a natural depression in the ground for a
campfire. Unhurriedly Frank takes a pot and fills it with water
from the lake. Every ounce of the lake water is fresh and sweet.
Then in a few easy forays he gathers dry wood for a fire—tender
dry twigs from fallen pine trees. A match-stroke later, the fire is
lighted, and a blazing flame licks at the soon-boiling water. Add
the rice, stir a little, slice the cheese, open a can of beans, and sup-
per is served. Frank eats heartily after a day's invigorating pad-
dling.

After supper it's time to relax. He props himself against a still-
warm rock and settles back to read a paperback with a cup of hot
drink by his side. He reads easily in the alternatively warm and
cool breezes of the evening, pausing every few moments to sip a
little of the warm drink. And at sunset he puts the book down for
a long look across the lake as the red-yellow rays of the sun
stretch warm shadows over the pine forest and across the lake to
his feet . . .

It was a perfect routine. A dream fulfilled. But there was
something terribly wrong with it. Only a few days into the
voyage, it hit him—the terrible loneliness. There were no people
out there. He was absolutely alone with his thoughts. Nobody to
share the sunset with. No one to hear his exclamations of wonder
at the geese winging in low formation over the canoe.

At first Frank felt alone and free. The solitude he craved was
upon him. Then he felt the stifling, tragic loneliness of total
isolation. It was a feeling so unexpected it took him by surprise
at first. Then, day by day, lonely week after lonely week, he
grappled with it, attempting to rationalize it away.

"I'm better off now than I've ever been in my whole life,"
Frank told himself somewhat untruthfully. He thought back over
his life. Against the white noise of solitude he played and

replayed his memories. Memories of all the crises from the past.

He remembered his anger against authority—unjust and unreasonable authority. He remembered his battle of wills with a father pushing authority to enforce what was best for a rebellious son. The military, medical school; the military, medical school flashed to mind alternately as he reviewed his life in detail.

And always there was Snesia. The tragic love of his previous life. His memories almost sighed with agony each time they brought her back—but he would have it no other way. Frank needed this dialogue of the soul to understand his grief.

This grief is selfish. This grief is selfish. The thought played itself over and over in his thoughts like a broken record day after day. Frank had so committed himself emotionally to Snesia that her absence left him without a goal. In all their trials and troubles, he aimed to encourage her, to make *her* happy. Now she was gone. He could do nothing for her, and all those impulses now turned inward in a dark self-pity.

"Oh, God," Frank anguished in his quiet misery, "what am I left with? I'm lonely and alone, with no one to share with."

In reality he was not yet reconciled to the fact that Snesia was gone. He held out the irrational idea that somehow, somewhere he would again meet up with her personality. Perhaps hear her husky voice again. Maybe look up and see her walking toward him through the trees. Frank needed to share his experiences with her, show her the lakes, paddle away with her to other adventures.

This expedition to the boundary waters was actually the logical follow-up to his life of unease, of loathing for city ways, of rebellion against the way things are in an imperfect society. Only his dedication to Snesia held him back when she was alive. He might have cut and run years earlier but for her. Now, ironically, her death had freed him from a world he no longer wanted to deal with. The government death benefits of over $400 a month more than supported his wilderness ways. Frank seldom needed more than half that amount. The rest he gave away as gifts to friends and relatives.

He had a desperate need to share. In earlier years he'd shared outdoor experiences with Snesia. Now that was impossible.

Many times in the past, Frank had returned from expeditions just bubbling over with things to relate, eager to tell others about what he'd seen, to show pictures and laugh about it all. That feeling was gone. Now it all seemed strangely flat. One day hardly stood out from another.

After several months alone on the lakes, Frank capitulated to the loneliness. He needed company—any company. He placed an advertisement in the Pittsburgh Explorers Club newsletter. "Available: guide for canoeing expeditions in boundary waters area. Contact Frank Kelly."

It wasn't long before he received a reply. Eldon Treadwell contacted him by phone after writing a note. "I'd like my wife Rachael to spend a few months on the lakes," he said. "She's been a bit stressed out lately, and I think it will do her good to get away from it all."

"Send her up," suggested Frank with hardly a moment's hesitation. Rachael and Snesia had known each other quite well. In fact, the Treadwells had joined them on about five club outings.

Rachael turned up in Ely soon after the call. She appeared hyperactive and overexcited about the trip to come. Frank remembered then, a little too late, that Rachael was a woman given to pretty violent mood swings. The next six months would be the greatest adventure of her life. Frank, too, would have cause to remember their travels.

The adventure began well enough. Together they paddled off again into the vast network of lakes and woodland in the boundary area. Day after day they shared the spectacles of nature. This may have been an area frequented in earlier days by French trappers, but left alone as it had been for many years, the area had recovered to a wonderful abundance. Beaver, otter, elk, moose, wolf, and other creatures abounded. All, of course, against the backdrop of quiet water and untouched forests.

That summer Frank and Rachael canoed over 1,100 miles along the boundary area. They traveled east along the *voyageur* waterways to Thunder Bay on Lake Superior. Stroke after paddle stroke they moved hundreds of miles around the northern edge of that huge lake, then on through the channel at its eastern end, and entered Lake Huron. Beyond they moved down through the north channel islands and across to the far eastern side of the lake.

Some days Rachael was an ideal companion. She was used to the outdoor life and eager to see as much of the lake wonders as she could. Often she went off exploring by herself while Frank set up camp or stayed back to repair their gear. After one such outing she came back very impressed by a chance meeting with a well-equipped canoeing party several miles away.

"You should have seen all the equipment," she told Frank later. "The canoes were loaded down with every gimmick and convenience you could imagine. And guides! It seemed that most of the party were guides."

"What was it all about?" asked Frank, a little curious.

"Well, it turned out they were out testing equipment for a big mail-order company. You'll never guess who was in charge of the expedition. Edmund Hillary—*the* Sir Edmund Hillary. The first man to climb Mount Everest in Nepal."

Frank was interested. Hillary was a folk hero among outdoor clubs.

"He asked me how long I'd been out," said Rachael. Of course he had. It was almost as common a greeting as Hello out on the lakes. The answer gave some indication of the type of person you were dealing with.

"I told him I had only been out a few weeks," said Rachael, "but that my guide—you—had been out for four months. He was impressed. Said you were a true outdoorsman. Too bad you couldn't meet him."

Such pleasant exchanges with Rachael soon became the exception. Any little incident tended to stir her up into a fury. At such times she would assume any one of about half a dozen personalities. One day she might be a little girl. Another day a mother personality. Then, just as quickly, she would assume the behavior of some teacher she had known. It didn't take Frank long to recognize her personality disorder. At first he found it disruptive; then later he began to fear for his safety.

Stopping at one little town along the way they took time out for a volleyball game with some locals. It was great fun and a good way to change pace after unbroken days of canoeing. Both Rachael and Frank enjoyed the rough-and-tumble interaction of the game.

After the game, Frank loaded up his pack and moved outside

the gymnasium with the players.

"Great game," commented one of the local boys. "Glad you guys could join us," he told Frank and Rachael. Then as an afterthought he added, "By the way, there's a social evening planned for tomorrow night. Why don't you come along?"

"Sure, we'll be there," agreed Frank easily.

"Oh, good," exclaimed one of several girls from the game. "There'll be dancing too," she said, giggling with her friends.

"Well, maybe you'll spare a dance for me, then," joked Frank in a bantering manner.

Wham! Rachael attacked him with fist and nails, kicking and clawing. In the blur of the first moment, Frank realized some misplaced jealousy had snapped her into a frenzy. Their volleyball friends looked on in amazement.

Rachael punched Frank in the face a few times before he could duck. She grabbed at his clothes, ripping away the front of his shirt and tearing the buttons loose. Frank attempted to laugh it off. "Hey, take it easy," he said; "I give up."

Stung to further fury, Rachael reached into her pack and pulled out a hunting knife. Frank sprang back out of range. Rachael knew what she was doing, though, and in several long slashes she cut open his down sleeping bag, which lay rolled up on his pack. It would be a very uncomfortable night. She smiled at him malevolently.

"Sorry, guys," said Frank apologetically to the others. "Maybe we'll give the social a miss." They walked away quickly, shaking their heads.

There were other personalities. This lady was quite capable of attacking him with a hatchet as he slept. Frank studied her condition almost in a clinical sense. In some ways their relationship became doctor and patient. He finally unlocked the cause to her trauma: as a child, Rachael had been sexually abused by her mother. That didn't make the all-night arguments any easier to take, however.

After four months, Frank decided enough was enough. He called Eldon in Pittsburgh and said, "Eldon, I am not going to baby-sit your wife anymore. You have to take her back home."

Eldon didn't seem too interested in that idea. "I don't know why she can't stay," he said. "Rachael is having a great time. In

letters and phone calls she tells me she's having the adventure of
her life."

Frank wasn't going to dodge the issue anymore. "Look, she
has mental problems. You know what they are." Silence. "I can't
stand her anymore."

"Let me talk to Rachael," was Eldon's answer.

Frank stood aside and let her talk for a while. When he picked
up the receiver again, Eldon had a proposal. "You're right," he
said. "Rachael is having problems. But I know the life up there is
helping her. I'll pay you to take care of her."

"OK," said Frank, determined to scare him off. "Let's sign a
contract."

"What's your price?"

"$1,000 for four months," answered Frank, certain it would
end the negotiations. Rachael was always tight with money, and
this would end it.

"We'll sign," said Eldon. "Draw up the contract, have Rachael
sign and send it to me."

Frank was afraid he might have sold his life too cheaply.

He rented a cabin fifty miles from Ely as a base for their continued exploration of the small lakes in the area. Too late, he
realized that he was basically locking himself up with a tigress.
Rachael now had something specific against him. In her eyes he
was a thief—a man out to take her money dishonestly. It ate at
her and led to some ugly scenes. Eldon may have promised the
$1,000 dollars, and at the time she may have agreed, but now
she wasn't going to pay. "You can't charge us that money," she
screamed in one of her more rational arguments. "I won't pay
you."

She never paid the money. Eldon sent the check, but Frank
never saw it. Rachael got to it first. They shared a common box
at a post office about three miles out of Ely. Frank went to ex-
traordinary lengths to guarantee he was there first. The night
before the priority-mail letter arrived, he walked out and
camped in front of the post office. Rachael also hiked out.
Frank was certain she spent the night in Ely, three miles
away.

The next morning Frank awoke well before the 8:00 a.m.
opening time. It was a late November morning and very cold. A

neighbor invited him to come in and warm himself for a few minutes by the stove. Fifteen minutes after the hour, Frank thanked him and walked across to claim his letter. Too late. Somehow Rachael had beaten him to it. The box was empty.

Thoroughly disgusted, Frank tramped back to town determined to have it out with her. He found her eating breakfast in a crowded restaurant.

"Give me that check," Frank demanded as he sat down at the table. "We have an agreement signed by you."

"Never," she yelled, attracting a little attention. "It's my money. I'll never give it to you."

"I'll sue you for the money," Frank threatened with feeling but little reality.

She flared, and for a few moments they exchanged threats. One of them must have touched the go button for her most bizarre behavior.

"*Ahhh . . .*" she screamed long and loud at the top of her voice. There was panic in the restaurant. People looked at Frank. Was he attacking the poor woman? Frank certainly did not look trustworthy. His beard was long and matted. His clothes, while serviceable, showed the wear and tear of months of wilderness living.

He had to get away before someone arrested him. Quickly he dashed outside the restaurant. Rachael followed him, screaming all the time.

Desperately, Frank lashed out at her verbally, warning her away. He never knew what it was he said, but it was enough. Rachael walked away. It was the last time he saw her.

The trek back to the cabin seemed even longer than fifty miles. Those early days on the lakes were so lonely he'd yearned for human company. That wish had turned into a nightmare. But was the solitude again any solution? He was apprehensive.

One night on the trail seemed straight out of a horror tale. Before making camp for the evening he accidentally surprised a bull moose—not an animal to be taken lightly. Frank scrambled off into the forest to escape the obviously belligerent animal. He heard it rushing through the bushes after him. Again he ran, pausing to rest and listen. After a long wait he heard the bull again, pushing closer in the gathering darkness.

All his fears embodied could scarcely have made for a more sleepless night.

Winter already sat heavily on the woods of northern Minnesota. The summer green had either faded and fallen or was now covered by snow. Frank felt like a sleepwalker in a ghostly land. He was walking away from civilization toward a silent, unhearing world. A cold and threatening world.

His emptiness was more than a feeling. Frank truly believed that something in him, his soul perhaps, died that day at Seneca Rocks. He was not really a human being anymore—rather, a ghost floating across the surface of the earth. All that remained was the husk of a man, an empty shell. The shell wandered aimlessly, and nothing held any significance anymore. Another low point.

It took a long time to warm the cabin. Eventually the stove heated up, and a sense of comfort returned to Frank's world. This was his oasis of comfort in a cold desert. Outside was the wilderness, province of fang and claw. Whenever he went outside the cabin for wood, there were fresh tracks of bear, wolf, and lynx in the snow.

In effect he was trapped in the cabin. Early winter is not a time to move around the backwoods and waterways of Minnesota. It may snow, or it may sleet—a dangerous, soaking cold. The ice is just beginning to freeze—too thick to canoe and far too thin to walk on. A time to stay in a warm place and wait out the winter.

The cabin was well stocked; Frank had seen to that. Neat cords of firewood nearby guaranteed a small envelope of heat all winter. Plenty of food inside the cabin: fuel of a different sort, again stacked neatly like firewood. And books—lots of paperback books. Without books Frank might think too much on the past. He needed books. He needed a steady diet of them. One a day, at least. Fuel for the mind. They, too, were stocked and stacked for consumption.

Each day after rising, Frank fed the warm stove till it pulsed red. Then he heated some water and prepared breakfast from the contents of several, often disparate, cans. He ate in comfort under the outwardly frosted gaze of blank windows.

After breakfast came reading time. He'd grab the next book off the stack and settle back on the couch to page it through.

Frank devoured the books at a steady pace. His home-cooked food he found rather uniformly bland. Nourishing, but without vigorous exercise to sharpen the appetite, Frank found it uninspired and tasteless.

The books, on the other hand, varied widely in the fare they offered. After much reading, Frank developed the rule of thumb that three-quarters of all books were pure trash—indigestive pulp. Of the remainder, some was of limited value, and the rest was the world's greatest and most nourishing literature. Like cans without labels, it is often a case of open and taste before you know what you're eating.

During the ever-shortening days of advancing winter, Frank ate his way through a mixed salad of reading. Many days, what he read only added to his burden of loneliness, deepened his sense of isolation from humanity. Many of the books he read only increased his revulsion for the corruption in society.

Then one day Frank reached out to the diminishing pile of books and discovered the writings of Dr. Thomas Dooley.

Dooley's was a life shaped by service for humanity.

In 1954 Communist forces swept down through Indochina and routed the colonial French armies. The Communists exacted swift vengeance on those who might have helped the European colonizers. Christians were a special target for their hatred. Terror-stricken refugees crowded all roads south. They pushed off hostile shores in unseaworthy crafts, escaping to the open sea and dangerous freedom.

Many of them made it to American naval vessels anchored somewhat helplessly beyond the battle. Lieutenant Thomas Dooley, a naval doctor aboard those ships in the China Sea, determined to help the refugees. He organized rescue parties to pick up the floundering refugees. Then, as the situation worsened, he traveled to Hawaii, where he convinced naval authorities to take direct action. He was commissioned to establish huge refugee camps in South Vietnam.

Thousands of refugees were helped, healed, and nurtured by Thomas Dooley and his team of medical assistants. Dooley found a special fulfillment in helping others. He determined to dedicate his life to easing the suffering in that sad corner of the world.

Released from naval service, Thomas quickly raised funds for his dream and headed back to the jungles of Laos to establish a series of clinics.

Then in August 1959, he was diagnosed as having terminal cancer. Returning to the U.S. for treatment, he was showered with awards and praises. Dooley cared little for recognition. The cancer, too, he dismissed as less important than the larger task of service that called him. Within a few months he returned to his beloved clinic in Laos. Thomas Dooley died caring for others. He was only thirty-four.

In the winter quiet of his lonely cabin, cut off from all contact with humanity, Frank Kelly read and pondered the words of Thomas Dooley.

In his suffering, Frank imagined a God grown silent, uninterested. His faith almost destroyed by anguish, he had dared to question God's ways, and retreated into the woods, the very province of the Creator, in a wild flight from responsibility.

Almost against his will, in spite of his anguish, Frank heard the call to worship. He read Thomas Dooley's testament to a Creator and knew it was true. Dooley wrote of "an awareness of God, of the great pattern of the universe, the similarity of all the world, the magnificence of the dense green jungle, the majestic cathedral-like colors of the rain-forest, the rapids and rivers flowing one into another. All this cries of a Creator; this speaks of God" (Dooley, *The Night They Burned the Mountain*, p. 113).

Dooley, too, recoiled from the cities. "For me," he wrote, "it is harder to know God in the tumult of plenty, in city traffic, in giant buildings, in cocktail bars, or riding in a car with a body by Fisher. But just as a maker is stamped on America's products, so is His stamp on all the universe" (*ibid.*).

Frank had only to open the door, look out and up at the stars in an untouched heaven; out and across at the white world of winter to sense the waiting presence of God. Waiting for a revival of faith and hope within His creature.

In his last book *The Night They Burned the Mountain*, Thomas Dooley wrote of his own battle with illness, the spectre of death, and of the faith that sustained him. He told of taping a Christmas message for listeners at home and reading a few lines from a card someone sent him.

Frank read those lines as a message to his heart. "Are you willing to admit," he read, "that probably the only good reason for your existence is not what you are going to get out of life but what you are going to put into it? To close your book of complaints against the management of the Universe and to look around for a place where you can sow a few seeds of happiness?" (Dooley, p. 93).

Alone in the winter snows Frank pondered the morning of his life. Certainly it was an empty life. Sure it had adventure, challenge, and freedom. It was also a lonely life. He had no one to share with, no one to dedicate himself to.

Dooley wrote of "The Fellowship of Those Who Bear the Mark of Pain," a concept taught him by his friend and mentor, Albert Schweitzer. The members of the fellowship, explained Dooley, are united by the common bond of physical pain and bodily anguish. They have a duty to reach out and help others in their battles with pain and anguish.

No, Frank was not alone. He shared the pain of loss, the pain of disillusionment, of hopelessness, at times, with millions of others around the world. Thomas Dooley used his medical skills to ease the pain of many around him. Frank, too, could reach out to others through medicine. Perhaps he was needed; perhaps he was necessary in the greater scheme of things.

There were other books to read in the days that followed. Frank looked them over with weary glance. Again and again he returned to the words of Thomas Dooley, words of faith and service. They steered him almost against his will.

Further into his stock of books, Frank encountered another call to service. Another doctor, William Walsh, told of reaching out to a desperately ill Third World from *A Ship Called Hope*. It was a story of idealistic doctors and nurses sailing into forbidden seas of ignorance. They manned a peacetime hospital ship dedicated to bettering the lot of sufferers around the world.

Frank read and reread the book, till the conviction caught firm hold on his imagination. Somehow, someway, he would dedicate himself to helping the unfortunate in some lonely corner of the world.

The solitude of the cabin felt more oppressive than ever

before. He had to leave. It was almost as though the walls were pushing in on him, squeezing him, finally expelling him from their oppression.

It was time to move a little closer to the company of humans. Out in the wilderness he was company only to the wolf howl and empty tracks in the morning.

So Frank loaded his pack, bolted the cabin against the vast emptiness, and turned toward the town of Ely, fifty miles away. In many ways the snow-muffled walk back toward town was much more than Frank realized. He told himself it was cabin fever—the isolation of winter that drew him back in. Actually it was a turning point. The winter of his soul was beginning to thaw, even though some of the coldest days still lay ahead.

Frank stomped crustily into an army surplus store on the main street of Ely and looked around. He needed some extra equipment to survive the cold. His warm down-lined clothing still worked fine. A hooded parka deflected all but the bitterest winds. His down sleeping bag was almost adequate, but just to be sure, he selected two army blankets for $4 each. Good insurance for chills in the night.

Rummaging through piles of surplus boots he came across a pair of felt-lined army boots. Most outdoorsmen scorned such boots. Leather boots cracked easily in the cold. Felt, however, was often worse. Often felt shoes cracked so badly that the soles fell off. Frank checked the boots over and decided they would do. The price was good. The secondhand dealer asked only $12 for them.

The next most pressing problem was shelter. Frank wasn't quite ready to crowd into town and pay rent. He still felt too much a part of the wilds. With a woodsman's eye he spied out the countryside near town and settled on a spot just a two-minute walk from the main street. Getting there was no easy matter, though.

Frank tailed off from the snow-packed avenue across empty lots and into the nearby woods. Beyond that, the area dropped off in a steep ice cliff. With the practiced skill of a mountaineer, he traced a way down the cliff onto the frozen lake surface below. There, off to one side in the shelter of some pine trees, Frank built his winter home.

Within no more than six hours he fashioned a sturdy snow cave. With machete and shovel he fashioned the hard-packed snow into a white, domed-shaped shelter from the coldest winds. Frank dragged his pack inside and set up house. The insulating snow kept out the worst of winter. Ground sheets, blankets, and sleeping bag ensured dry and warm comfort for cold evenings. It was the ultimate in low-cost, practical housing.

Each day Frank began a ritual: exit his cave, climb up the cliff, walk into the town of Ely and along the streets to the local college library. It was warm there, and he was drawn to the warmth. He was also drawn to the books. They were his link to the larger world of ideas, of dreams, of action.

Each evening he returned to his snow cave to eat a meal warmed on a small stove and to sleep in tomblike quiet among the cold crystals. The routine became so familiar he almost ceased to think on the details.

Then one night he returned in a blowing snowstorm to find the cave empty. It took several moments for the reality to sink in. Someone had entered his private world while he was away, violated it, and stolen his belongings. More than mere theft, the encroachment threatened his very survival.

The sleeping bag was gone, along with most of the other items in the cave. He scratched around in the snow in a quick panic. Yes, the thief also took the last few reminders of his wife.

It was too late in the evening to go for help, or revenge. Besides, what would anyone do? At the very least they would laugh at his foolishness for shunning a town to live in the ice like some winter worm.

Frank sat the night out in the cave. His down clothes kept out the killing cold, but it was too cold to sleep. It was a time to think, to reflect on his life, the futility of the adventure, the reason for his flight to solitude. He thought of Snesia, his battles with authority and society, his awakening desire to dedicate his life to service.

In the morning he tramped stiffly to town. The first item of business: buy a new sleeping bag and replacements for the rest of his camping gear. That done, he went to the local newspaper office and placed an advertisement. It was an open note to the person or persons responsible for the theft. It was both practical and plaintive. "Please return my passport," the note requested. "And please return the remembrances of my wife that you stole—they are my dearest possessions."

"Run that ad till I get a reply," Frank directed the lady at the ad counter.

Whoever stole the goods knew where his snow cave was. There was no point in returning. He had to find a new and more secure spot for a second snow cave.

This time Frank followed the trail out of town for about five minutes before settling on a spot. Near a railroad track he came upon a clump of thick, low-lying pine trees. He found that by leaping from the embankment onto the trees he was able to disguise his tracks. Behind the trees he set to work building another snow cave. It was the perfect spot. His cave was totally invisible to passersby. Frank had only to leap out from the trees onto the road.

It was a new routine, this leap from the brushes out onto the road. From there on, it was unchanged. Every day Frank traveled to the library to read and study.

Ely, on the edge of forest land, is somewhat of a frontier town. Residents are used to outdoor types, men in rough clothing. Among them Frank still stood out as somewhat unique. Long hair, wild beard, faded clothing with many signs of rough repair, and, of course, the secondhand felt boots. At first the librarian looked at him sharply, worried he might create a scene in the library. Eventually, they spoke, and she found him an educated, even personable, visitor. The emptiness in his eyes told her that he needed the calm of the library to reestablish his commerce with society.

Eight days after the theft, Frank found a note in his box at the post office. "I have your things," it read. It was signed "Vance Hanks."

Vance was the local lowlife, a Vietnam veteran emotionally scarred by the experience and unable to hold down a job. Often in trouble with the police, Vance lived with his alcoholic wife in a tumbledown shanty on the outskirts of Ely.

The note gave Frank a focus for his indignation. He strode down the alleys to Vance's cabin and pounded on the door.

"It's Frank Kelly," he yelled with a touch of anger. "I've come to get my things." He heard the bolt pull, and the badly fitting door opened till it jammed in the frozen drift. A bearded face peered out at him. The eyes squinted in snowy sunlight. "Come on in, Frank," invited Vance. "I've been expecting you."

Inside, the hut was dark, and the air smelled of cheap wine. "Sit down on the sofa," invited Vance, dignifying the battered lump of cushions to which he pointed.

Frank was a little angered by Vance's civility, as though he had just come to visit, to socialize. This was the home of the man who had robbed him.

Vance saw the signs of hostility and held up his hands as if in self-defense. "Look, man," he said, "I'm with you on what you're doing."

"What do you mean?" shot back Frank.

"I mean, saying to hell with it all, getting out of the rat race, and living in the woods by yourself. I can dig that, man."

Frank felt an unspeakable revulsion at the comradely way this detritus spoke to him. No way were they on the same wavelength. He looked into Vance's troubled eyes. This man was a danger to himself. He looked at Vance's appearance—scruffy and unkempt. Vance was unfit for normal society. He was a thief, an alcoholic, and an antisocial misfit. One of the walking wounded from a war Frank hated.

"Why did you take my gear?" Frank challenged aggressively, wanting to cut away the amiability.

"I had to, Frank." Vance put on a friendly air. "I was out snow-mobiling on the lake one day when I noticed this group of boys dragging stuff out of a snow cave on the bank."

"Yes," said Frank, sure there was more.

"Well, I chased them away, of course. It was obvious they were up to no good. So I loaded everything in the cave on to my snow-mobile and brought it back here for safekeeping. I saved your stuff, man."

The explanation was only half-plausible.

"I spent that night sitting in the cave with no sleeping bag. It was ten degrees below that night," said Frank, almost as a challenge.

"I'm sorry. You've got to believe I intended to give it all back to you." Vance seemed to actually crave the role of do-gooder.

"People got the wrong idea about me," he said. "I would never steal from a guy like you."

"Where is my gear?" demanded Frank.

"It's here," said Vance, going to a rough closet and bringing out a bundle wrapped in the sleeping bag. "Everything's here, including those things belonging to your wife."

Frank checked the pile over. Yes, it was all there. He picked it up and moved to the door. Vance followed him, almost fawning in a last attempt to build common ground.

"I'm with you," he said.

Frank walked out into the street with his bundle. His anger had changed to fear. What if Vance were right? Were they brothers in lifestyle? He looked back at Vance one last time: unkempt, undisciplined, fulfilling no useful function in the world.

Not too long after that, Frank placed a long-distance call to Huntington, West Virginia.

"Hello, Frank," boomed the medical director. "It's been a long time. So good to hear from you. We've missed you."

"I've been thinking," Frank said, hoping the director's friendship was more practical. "I've been thinking it's about time I picked up on medicine again."

"Yes," said the voice expectantly.

"Well, what I'm really asking is, do you have a need for a resident at the VA hospital right now?"

"Of course we do, Frank," laughed the director, having put Frank through the test. "The moment I answered the phone I intended to ask you to come. We have a vacancy right now. You'll be making my job a lot easier by coming. We've had trouble keeping residents lately."

"I'll be on the job in a few days," Frank proposed. "Thanks again."

Next stop, the Greyhound ticket office. He couldn't wait to get back into medicine. His excitement had something to do with a book in the cabin and a few lines of poetry from Robert Frost the author quoted.

> The woods are lovely, dark and deep.
> But I have promises to keep,
> And miles to go before I sleep.

13

A HALF-HEARTED TRY

*D*on't worry, madam," Frank reassured. "Johnny will be just fine: I'll see to that." He patted the ten-year-old boy on the back in his most fatherly, professional manner and continued, "Just a little ear infection, that's all."

The mother looked at him with trusting eyes. "Thank you, Doctor; it is so good to know Johnny is under your care."

Frank reached for his pen and wrote out a prescription with a confident hand. "Make sure Johnny takes this medication twice a day," he instructed. "Then come back in a week, and we'll check up on this young man . . ." Johnny sat up in his chair and smiled. ". . . just to see if everything cleared up as it should."

"Thank you, Doctor," said Johnny's mother with happy tears of relief.

"Take care of your mother, Johnny," said Frank with a playful tap to the boy's shoulder. "See you both next week."

Mother and son left the office smiling. "That Dr. Kelly is a wonderful man," announced the woman to the nurse as she signed out. "You must count it a privilege to work with him."

The Dr. Kelly who left Huntington VA hospital nearly two and a half years earlier had changed. Back then, Dr. Kelly just put his time in and nothing more. He had been arrogant and unmindful of what others thought. He had felt no need to especially hurry to the emergency room, and when he did show up he looked grim and gave short, curt answers. That was then.

The new Dr. Kelly wanted to help, went out of his way to show concern for patients.

Whenever a patient called with a question serious or simple, he was available and pleasant. He spoke sincerely to worried family members, almost as one of the family himself. And when summoned to the emergency room he answered promptly, appropriately flushed from the hurry of getting there. Frank Kelly enjoyed making people feel better. He had determined to apply himself to the healing profession.

Many things had changed at Huntington VA. Frank's immediate supervisor was now a Dr. Eglinda. He knew her from medical school days. They were not friends, however. Far from it. Dr. Eglinda was a strict and opinionated woman who believed that most of the male doctors were incompetent. Frank discovered that she had already forced two of the male residents to leave the hospital. Very quickly he realized she intended to add him to that list.

"Watch out for Dr. Eglinda," warned one of the nurses. "She keeps a list of your mistakes to show you are incompetent."

The first time he heard the warning, Frank felt culpable. After all, he'd been away from medicine for well over two years. He was pretty rusty in some areas. Of course, he made mistakes. But he was applying himself, and it was only a matter of time till he picked it all up again.

"Dr. Eglinda is on your case, Frank," commented a fellow resident a few weeks later. "She asked me to report any slips you make. I think she is keeping a list. You'd better keep your wits about you. She's already forced two doctors to leave."

Frank thanked him for the advice and went right back to doing his best for the patients. In earlier years he might have challenged Dr. Eglinda, fought hard against her chauvinism. He certainly would have worried himself sick over the conflict. Little things, petty worries consumed him in those other days. A phone bill would lead to worries over finances, an interrupted study session to agonies over a possible low grade. The new Frank Kelly was almost uncaring of such concerns.

"Why aren't you worried, Frank?" asked a nurse one day after she told him of further plans to blacklist him.

"I'm doing my best," answered Frank. "I'm helping patients; that's my real reward."

"Eglinda just may succeed in sending you packing, Frank," warned the nurse.

"Maybe it would be for the best," said Frank. "I don't intend to stay here forever. Eventually I'm going to practice medicine in the Third World, where doctors are really needed."

"She may force you out before you're ready to leave," persisted the nurse, impressed, just the same, by Frank's determination to go to the Third World.

"It won't matter," dismissed Frank. "I've learned not to worry about things like that. If it came to that, I'd just put my pack on my back and walk out of here."

Talk like that usually mystified his hearers. The nurse walked away shaking her head. She hoped it would not come to that.

"To the emergency room, quickly," called another nurse. "They need you there right away, Dr. Kelly."

Frank raced down to the emergency area. Several nurses were gathered around a still form.

"What's the story?" he asked breathlessly.

Briefly the paramedic filled him in on the basics of the case. It seemed pretty routine, even though the patient appeared gravely ill. Frank quickly scratched a prescription onto a pad. "Give this to him in the exact dosage and let me know of any change in the patient's condition."

Several hours later a tight-lipped colleague approached him with grave news. "Your patient in the emergency room just died," he announced. "It looks like you misdiagnosed the problem. Eglinda is investigating. Things look bad, Frank. She is saying you're incompetent and that she'll see you leave."

Things were every bit as bad as Frank's colleague feared. A little later he was summoned for a conference with Dr. Eglinda and the medical director.

"You've just killed a patient," accused Dr. Eglinda.

"It seems you were a bit hasty, Frank," said the director, not wanting to come down strongly on either side.

"Sir, you know my abilities," reminded Frank. "I'm more competent than most. The only case Dr. Eglinda has against me is that I'm a bit rusty from my time away."

The director sighed and turned to pace behind his desk. Frank realized the man would give in to Eglinda. He hated conflict, and she could give it double measure.

"See this paper?" said Dr. Eglinda, waving a handwritten form under his nose. "This is a signed statement from the director of the emergency room, outlining your incompetence and recommending that you be released from your responsibilities at this hospital."

Frank looked at the signature. "But this man does not even know me," he said. "He was not there when I treated the patient."

The director looked quizzically at Dr. Eglinda. "Is that really true?" he asked.

". . . as well as that statement, I have a report, signed by a number of nurses, that clearly indicates Dr. Kelly is incompetent."

The director looked at Frank for the next move. "I've been planning to leave for quite a while," said Frank. "I intend to practice medicine overseas." Barely six months had passed since Frank had returned to Huntington.

Nurse April Glendower was particularly upset that Frank might be leaving. She had known Snesia, and perhaps, unconsciously, that was why Frank continued to seek her out. Their friendship deepened into something that April felt was a little more.

"Don't leave me, Frank," she implored when she saw that he was serious about taking to the back trails again. "I'll go with you, anywhere."

"All right, then," said Frank, flattered by her professed devotion. "Let's sell everything. Give up your job, and we will travel all around the United States and Canada. I'll show you some fantastic sights."

Surprisingly, April followed through. She quit her job and sold most of her possessions. Then she picked up Frank and his pack in her car. Another great adventure had begun.

Five days into the trip, however, April began to think better of her decision. Hard hiking and sleeping out on mountain trails were not quite the free and easy life she had imagined.

"I can't stand it anymore," she said one day as they hiked back to the car in a gently falling rain. Frank couldn't quite understand her frustration. After Minnesota this was almost tropical.

"It's been days since I bathed," April whined. "You may like to live like a ruffian, but this is definitely not the life for me." She kept up the complaining all the way back to the car. They argued a bit more over the life Frank lived. Frank told her a shower a day and fresh clothes were not necessarily tops on his list of outdoor necessities.

April was fed up. Finally, she flung open the car door and announced curtly, "I am going back, OK?" Frank picked up his pack and walked back up the trail. Behind him he heard the engine start up, revving wildly. The tires screeched as April sped away. Soon she was gone, and the quiet of the trail fell back around Frank.

It was another turning point for Frank. Snesia had fulfilled his life in so many ways that her death left him empty and vulnerable. The faces may have belonged to other women, but in each case he was subconsciously searching for Snesia. Snesia was the one who shared his outdoor dreams; Snesia was the one prepared to leave family and home forever to live with him. Snesia was the woman who, believing in this life only, chose to live it with him.

After April left, Frank realized more clearly that it was impossible to recapture Snesia through another human being. The answer to his continuing restlessness was not another woman. It was not even within himself. But that knowledge was only to come much later.

Frank hiked along the Appalachian Trail in North Carolina for a few days before deciding to head west. Those caches of food and equipment would prove handy now that he was roaming again. He made his way to the nearest small town and bought a cheap bus ticket to Biggs, Oregon.

"Where are you off to, fellow?" asked a seatmate at one point as the bus droned its way along the interstate.

"Oh, out west," said Frank.

"You look like you have hiking in mind," the elderly gentleman persisted.

"Yes," answered Frank, prodded to more detail. "I may spend some time hiking along the Pacific Crest Trail in Oregon."

The man looked out the window with wistful eyes. "I always wanted to cut loose and investigate this country at my own pace," he said. "Just never got around to it. What with a farm to keep up and a family to raise. The years just ran on by, without my noticing it." He turned back to Frank. "How long are you planing to spend on the trail?"

Frank wasn't quite prepared for that question. "Oh . . . oh, a few weeks maybe."

"Yes, I know what you're feeling," said the old farmer. "There's always the pull of home. Won't be long before you're ready to pack up and head back home with stories to tell and things to share with your family. Living ain't no fun without sharing, is it?"

14

A LONELY
MOUNTAIN HOME

*B*iggs, Oregon, at last! The bus coasted rapidly into the terminal, air brakes pulsating rapidly. With a final pneumatic wheeze the doors snapped open, and Frank stepped stiffly out onto the pavement. He looked across the wide Columbia River toward the distant Cascade Mountains. Time to start hiking again. Frank pulled his pack from the luggage area under the impatiently growling bus and strode away. One item of business to take care of, and then he'd be on his way to the freedom of the Pacific Crest Trail.

Well out of town Frank scanned for familiar landmarks. Yes, there was the rock and the old tree stump. He took out his camp shovel and began digging. Five feet down he struck the garbage can. A few minutes later, and he was in possession of all the cached supplies. He now had all the camping gear and food he needed to tackle a few weeks on the trail.

Once across the Columbia River, Frank struck out northward toward the high mountain peaks.

Climbing ever higher on the trail, he seemed to be free of the pull of the past. The thin air seemed to clear his mind of further questions of Why? and What next? By day the tall peaks kept sentinel watch—off to his left rose mighty Mt. Rainier and close by the trail, the slightly smaller challenge of Mt. Adams. By night the silent and secure stars looked down on his solitary campsite. It should have been the ultimate escape.

After only a few days on the trail, however, Frank began to literally feel the weight of his isolation. For the most part, the trail largely bypassed towns and resupply spots, so he needed to carry at least three weeks' worth of supplies with him. Those supplies translated into quite a heavy load. It soon became a crushing load. Maybe Frank was out of condition. Maybe he felt the weight because there was no challenge to spur him on. Maybe he was lonely.

He began to long for comforts the trail couldn't provide. *Oh boy*, he thought one day, *what I wouldn't give for a bowl of homemade granola.* Not the expensive, commercial variety, but the rich, homemade variety he used to put together in Minnesota. *All I need are the basic ingredients, a frying pan, a stove—and, of course, a cabin.* Yes—he needed a cabin, a home to stop in, to rest in, to settle down in. Maybe he'd buy some land and build that cabin.

After three weeks of lonely hiking, Frank hit a main highway. The trail continued across to the other side, up and away north. He stopped by the side of the highway and thumbed down a truck heading west to Seattle. He had a plan.

"Got family in Seattle?" asked the driver as they motored down the highway.

"No," answered Frank. "I'm not staying there. Just passing through." He almost wished he could tell the trucker that Seattle was home.

"Too bad," said the driver, downshifting quickly to hold the truck back on the rapid descent from the Cascades to the coast. "I'm from Seattle. It's home to me. I'm looking forward to getting back and spending a few days with the family. I've been on the road too long," he said with a quick glance at Frank's worn pack propped up on the seat against the door.

Once in Seattle, Frank headed to the nearest bicycle shop. He quickly picked out a sturdy model with plenty of add-ons to carry camping gear. He was in a hurry to find that block of land, to find a spot for a cabin, a place to call home.

The road headed north, and Frank followed it on the bicycle. He explored every detour that appealed to him. He poked into every quiet corner of the mountain recesses, hoping to find the perfect spot to pause for longer than an overnight pitch. That spot began to seem elusive.

He turned east on Highway 20 and cycled with ever more labored pedal strokes up into the high Cascades again. At Marblemount, Frank turned off the highway and moved more easily up a deep valley. The farther he traveled into its closeted grandeur, the more Frank became convinced that this was the place.

Finally, he found it. Deep in the valley, nestled close against the side of a 5,000-foot mountain and surrounded by tall stands of pine trees, a vacant lot with a For Sale sign beckoned him. Frank knew at once this was his spot. To him the sign said "home." Time to start building that cabin.

At first glance the valley appeared almost uninhabited. Cycling into the close confines of the green valley, Frank had noticed an occasional cabin or two among the trees. But he still basically believed he was at the outer reaches of human settlement. It was indeed an isolated valley, but it was hardly uninhabited. From the day he signed for the little one-seventh acre lot, Frank discovered an ever-widening world of friendly neighbors.

"Welcome to the valley," said the man driving the truckload of logs from the sawmill. "I'm your neighbor down the way." He gestured toward a distant slope of the valley. "Where do you want the logs?" Frank told him, the logs were dropped, and the driver lingered for quite a while to chat. Finally he climbed back into the cab and waved goodbye. "Just holler if you need anything," he said, and drove off. Frank attacked the work at hand. It was good to be welcomed this way, and he noted the fact that the man asked few questions about his past. In time he found that many of his neighbors were refugees of one sort or another, just like himself—loners and free spirits.

The summer went by quickly in a blur of building, meeting new acquaintances, and, of course, long treks into the surrounding wilderness. Frank needed the lone breaks to clear his head and keep one step ahead of any bothersome memories.

Winter comes early in the high Cascades. By the time Frank finished the cabin, snow lay white around the freshly cut walls, and winter storm clouds swirled low over the surrounding mountains. He lighted up the wood-burning stove for the first time, savoring the warm glow. There'd be lots of granola this winter. Granola and warm cheer would keep him over the cold spell.

Newfound friends stopped by to chat now and then. Frank would throw an extra log on the fire, and they'd talk late into the night.

Then when the sky cleared a little, Frank bundled up and went outside to tramp the woods and climb the high snow peaks. He still loved the challenge of beating the elements, of tackling whatever nature could throw out.

But as the cold days shortened, Frank realized that his newfound world was again turning into something less than satisfying. The mountains never let up on him. They were always there—towering above the cabin, hedging him in. Inside the cabin he was warm, but a prisoner of sorts. Friends came to visit and talk, but the conversation seemed to accentuate the involuntary hibernation.

Frank sat down one night and wrote a letter to his old climbing buddies in Pittsburgh—his friends in the Explorers Club. He'd written to them sporadically over the years, never really losing contact. This letter was a little different.

The words he wrote said one thing, but the timing said another. It said: "*I want out. I'm ready for another adventure. I need another challenge.*"

Writing the letter gave Frank more excuses to get out of the cabin. He trekked down to the distant country post office and sent the letter on its way east. He trekked back to the post office quite a few times before any letter came back.

When the postmaster handed him the letter postmarked "Pittsburgh," Frank ripped it open on the spot and devoured the contents. "The Explorers Club is organizing an expedition to Nepal early next year," he read. "We'd love to have you join our group. Can we count you in?" Did they really need to ask? Of course he would go! Climbing the high peaks of Nepal—land of the mighty Himalayas—was the ultimate aim of every mountaineer.

Frank penned an immediate reply and then almost ran through the snow back to his cabin. His thoughts were in a fever pitch of planning. There were so many details to take care of the next few weeks—visas, tickets, equipment.

"I'll be gone for almost ten weeks," Frank told neighbors who dropped in to visit from time to time. "I'm going to Nepal, where the mountains are almost too tall to climb." They were new but good friends. None of them remarked on the fact that only three months after finishing his cabin, a "permanent home" in the wilderness, he was off to a distant adventure. More than a few of them felt their own yearnings to escape to other valleys, so they said nothing.

The day he left the cabin, Frank took one last look around the familiar valley home. His eyes took in the cozy interior, the still-warm stove and rough-hewn cupboards stocked with nourishing food—and granola. Outside, he looked up once more past the gigantic pines around the cabin, up to the high peak of the mountain. It was cold, white, and yet a scene he had grown to love. Well, ten weeks would pass all too quickly, and he'd be back with tales to tell valley visitors.

He pulled the door shut without locking it. Removing his gloves for a moment he pinned a note to the door. "I'm gone for a little while," it read. "There's food and a stove inside; go ahead and enjoy yourself. Be back soon." He pulled his gloves back on and turned down the track toward the main road. His pack never seemed lighter.

15

THE LAST MOUNTAIN

*L*ong before the plane reached Nepal, Frank saw the Himalayan peaks floating toward them like rows of sharks' teeth atop the waves of clouds. Sharp and white, they looked improbably high and menacing.

Then the plane sank beneath the clouds on the approach to Kathmandu, and the mountains disappeared. The jet bucked and writhed as it descended between the hidden slopes. Its engines alternately whined in terror and quieted ominously. A final jolt, and they were below the cloud line. Frank looked out at the wide Kathmandu Valley below him. From above, it merited the Shangri-La legends.

The green valley floor stretched out flatly for miles around the city, until it met the surrounding mountains, which encroached irregularly by means of low, twisting ridges. Around the city small farm plots and rows of stone houses along the many streams broke the surface into a pleasing mosaic. The city itself, he saw, was not large, but a compact cluster of three- and four-storied buildings made of rough brick and carved wood.

A few moments more, and the plane swept into the airport. It landed with a thud. The pilot braked hard and swung the craft around at the end of the runway to taxi back to the simple single-story terminal.

The moment Frank walked down the ramp onto the tarmac, he knew this was another world. Behind the wire fence he saw a jostling crowd of Nepalese. His side of the fence was guarded by khaki-clad police.

Memories of Greyhound bus stations flooded over him inside the terminal. Baggage from the plane lay strewn all over the terminal area. It was every man for himself.

Frank retrieved his pack and lined up to have his passport checked and stamped by the one customs officer. Outside, the crowd babbled and yelled in Nepali, surging now and then through the barrier ahead of them, only to be prodded back by the police. When he finally inched his way to the booth, the officer leafed idly through the passport and stamped it without looking at him.

"Over here, Frank." It was the voice of Gary, one of his friends from Pittsburgh. A hand gestured in his direction above the pressing crowd. "Over here!"

Frank pushed through the imploring porters, taxi drivers, and beggars. Gary finally appeared in front of him. "It's wild, isn't it?" he said, shaking Frank's hand. "Great to see you. The others are waiting in town. We leave for the Kali Gandaki Trail tomorrow."

"How many made the trip?" asked Frank, raising his voice above the noise in order to communicate.

"Twelve, counting you," answered Gary. "Quite a group. You probably knew already that John Irving is with the group." Frank scowled. No, he didn't. Gary noticed his response. "John has been pretty free with his opinions of you," he said. "When he found out you were coming, he muttered something about 'I don't even want to be in the same country with that Frank Kelly.' "

"Well, I'll keep out of his way, then," promised Frank, not as ready to fight as in the old days.

"This way," Gary ordered suddenly as a beat-up taxi pulled alongside. He opened the door, and they both scrambled inside. Once on the road he turned to Frank again. "Then you don't know of the plan to climb Amadablan?"

"No," said Frank, suddenly interested.

"After our three-week trek, John plans to take a small team and tackle the mountain."

"Well, he sure won't want me on the same mountain," guessed Frank. Gary didn't answer.

They met up with the rest of the group at a downtown guesthouse. Most of them were old friends, climbing buddies on many earlier expeditions. Frank was bearhugged and backslapped from one to another. Then it was time to sit down on the grassmat floor, spread a map of Nepal on the low table, and go over the plans for the trek to Kali Gandaki.

Team members bantered and laughed together, excited by the upcoming adventure. It was as though nothing had changed. Only now and then did Frank catch some of his friends looking at him pensively. Most of them had known Snesia. Seeing Frank again reminded them of her absence. Five years is not a long time to dear friends.

From Kathmandu the team traveled 100 bumpy miles by bus to Pokhara, jump-off point for the trek. The township of Pokhara sits close by tranquil Lake Phewa Tal and beneath the shadow of the Annapurna mountain range—nearly 28,000 feet high.

Terraced fields of rice, millet, and corn stepped down to the shores of the lake itself. Nearby Frank saw pilgrims offering food before shrines at a Hindu temple. Bell tones of mystical music wafted though the thin air, mixed in harmony with birds' songs from high in the leafy swami trees. Merchants in narrow-fronted booths sat crosslegged, surrounded by their entire inventory, sometimes calling out to passersby, sometimes haggling loudly with customers. Above the narrow streets the brick buildings rose several stories to grass-covered tile roofs that protruded over finely carved wooden eaves. Every window frame was a work of fine wood-carving art. Gentle, smiling Nepalese followed the trekking team as it moved through town. Throngs of young children moved close, one even tugging on the straps of Frank's pack.

That was when he first began to notice the other side of the quaint beauty around him. The barefooted boy who tugged at Frank's pack reached out a thin arm and cried for "rupee." He was a beggar. His sad, stoic little face spoke of real need and suffering. The clothes he wore were dust colored more from dirt than dye.

Frank looked around with a new awareness. Streams of raw sewage ran between the worn cobblestones of the ancient streets. Another young child nearby stood watching through pus-filled eyes, every few moments drawing a bare arm across an upper lip streaked by flowing mucus. A grotesquely crippled beggar crept up the street toward the group, propelling himself like some stick-legged insect, hand already out toward them. "Rupee."

Outside the town they walked along a narrow road bordered on both sides by tangled bushes and the debris of a thousand trekking parties. Now and then an ancient bus would come lurching by at high speed. Invariably there were passengers on the roof and hanging from the doorways. The busses never swerved to avoid pedestrians, although the Nepalese on the road seemed slow to move out of the way.

Most of the traffic on the road consisted of pedestrians. Nepalese men with peaked caps and in traditional garb of dark vest and billowing skirt hanging low over tapered cotton trousers trudged stoically down the middle of the road. Sometimes they stopped to talk—squatting down in the middle of the road, rising only at the last minute to avoid any motorized traffic. Only a few of them paused to stare at the twelve Americans moving purposefully toward Kali Gandaki.

Beyond the subtropical Pokhara Valley the road diminished rapidly to a well-worn track. It rose in looping curves up the sides of the valley. Far below, Frank saw the small figures of women wading through the terraced rice paddies. Even from the distance it was obvious they were bent over and working the crop. He remembered noticing the calloused hands in the marketplace.

Evenings on the trail became a daily wonder. At almost every stop they were able to look out and see the stark and high peaks of the Annapurna range. At nightfall when the deep shadows fell over lower valleys and evening seemed to have arrived, the high mountains still shone in sunlit glory.

One night the group camped on a broad green meadow known as the Austrian Camp. Tall green trees kept their distance from the emerald green grasses of the high hillside. As always the horizon went no farther than the snow-white peaks of the Annapurnas. In many ways the scene resembled its Austrian namesake, making it an excellent set for *The Sound of Music,* should there ever be a remake. Around a campfire in a loose cluster of tents, the twelve friends shared their thoughts of the day.

"It's an amazing place," said Fred Edwin, a lawyer and the oldest of the group. "It's so removed from the real world." He threw a branch on the fire.

"No wonder the Nepalese worship some of these mountains," added another team member from behind the glowing embers of the campfire.

"It will be hard when we have to return to Pittsburgh," said Gary, looking away to the still-shining peaks.

Frank stared into the fire's burning center, thinking hard about what he would do after it was over.

"Is it back to the cabin after this, Frank?" asked another voice out of the dark.

"Maybe," replied Frank. "Maybe not." He thought deeply for a moment before he continued. He was aware of all the others watching him intently. "I've done a lot of thinking the past few years. Many times I decided I was better off away from society. You know, all the hassles, the corruption, pollution and so on." He saw a few nods beyond the fire. "Somehow my life has lost any meaning. I cross the boundary waters, I travel the Pacific Crest Trail, come to Nepal, and after it's over . . . I get this empty feeling again. What's it all for?"

"We understand, Frank," Fred's voice came from the shadows. "Snesia was very dear to us too. Life must go on, though."

"Yes, at first it was Snesia's death," agreed Frank. "I'll never forget her, but it goes beyond losing her. I hated God at first; now, that seems a little childish. I know He's out there somewhere, even though I can't touch Him."

The others were a little too embarrassed to discuss God openly. Frank continued. "Sometimes I feel like an empty husk. Like I'm just floating through the world; like I don't even belong here. Somehow I have to justify my existence. It's not enough to go on adventures; I know that now. I have to add something to the world."

The last rays of light were fading from Annapurna as he paused a long moment and continued.

"A while back I determined to go back into medicine, but it didn't work. One doctor more or less in the U.S. doesn't really make much difference. Then I thought, what about the Third World? Maybe I could bring help to needy people there."

"Great idea," agreed several of his listeners.

"I applied for work in South America," explained Frank. "That fell through. I don't really know what I will do now." There was nothing more to say.

Finally Gary reached out and put his hand on Frank's shoulder. "We are with you," he said. "For now let's get a good night's sleep. We've a long way to go tomorrow. Everything looks better after a good night's sleep."

Frank enjoyed the trek. He enjoyed the company of old friends on the trail. With them he gasped in pleasure at the succession of memorable moments. Other nights he laughed around the fire and shared the warmth. Back in his tent, though, it was cold, and his thoughts returned over and over to the meaning of his life.

Inevitably the trail led back to Kathmandu. After three weeks in the mountains and pack rations, the minimal comforts of a city seemed rich. At high altitudes water boils more slowly, and even simple cooking becomes a chore. In Kathmandu again, team members headed for a local restaurant. The basic economy and a nonconvertible rupee guaranteed a very good meal for just a dollar or two.

Frank and most of the other eleven filed into a likely looking second-floor restaurant in the Tamil section of town and ordered a meal. Spicy smells wafting from the back room promised it would be tasty.

"Hard to believe the trek is over," sighed one of the young doctors, thinking of glorious days on the trail.

"Yes, only a few days till we head back," added someone else. "Those lucky guys with John get to stay a few more weeks, though. I'd give anything to climb Amadablan with them."

"Back to the old grind for most of us," the first doctor added.

"What are your plans, Frank?" asked Gary.

"Nothing in particular," shrugged Frank.

At that moment the waiter came in with a steaming saucer of lentils and rice. For a few moments they moved the saucer around the low benches, each taking a big helping.

Gary turned to Frank again once the saucer was empty. "You must have some plan," he pursued, hoping to snap him into something specific. "There must be something you intend to accomplish."

"Well, I had a plan, but it's come to nothing," said Frank, not eager to go over his thoughts again. He didn't want to appear self-pitying and self-centered.

"Oh, you mean the plan to go to the Third World as a doctor," remembered Fred. "It's a great idea, Frank. Go for it. It's about time you stopped grieving and took a hold of yourself. Go to the Third World and do your bit."

"How about here, Frank?" suggested Gary. "You mentioned South America, but why not Nepal?"

"Why not Nepal?" the others chorused.

Why not, indeed! It was staring him in the face. Nepal obviously needed doctors. Maybe his friends were right. Just the same, it was an impractical idea. He knew of no contacts in Nepal, no way of even beginning to find them.

"Hey, look at this, will you!" One of the party leaned in through the door. "I think Frank should come and read this notice in the hallway." He was insistent, so Frank slid out from under the table to go see.

"Talk about a coincidence!" exclaimed the friend.

Frank's pulse quickened involuntarily as he read the neatly lettered handwritten sign. "We need volunteer doctors and nurses at Scheer Memorial Hospital, Banepa. This mission hospital has a warm, loving atmosphere among its staff. Contact Medical Director Dr. Vigna."

Others in the group had followed him into the hallway. They read the sign with enthusiasm. "This is fantastic. This is your chance, Frank," said Gary. "Check it out."

Frank reached up and pulled the notice free of the wall. Yes, he would check it out.

"Banepa," said one of the group, "where's that?"

"Not far, I think," said Fred, pulling out a hiking map. "Here it is. About twenty miles east of Kathmandu." He studied the contours on the map. "Looks like it's up in the hill area. Should be a nice spot."

"I'm going to check it out," announced Frank, not much caring where the hospital was.

"There should be a local bus to Banepa at the main depot," someone suggested as Frank moved toward the door.

"Banepa?" he asked at the dusty downtown bus terminal. Eventually a taciturn Nepalese pointed to one of the native buses. "Banepa," he said.

The bus was not large. A vehicle its size might normally carry about sixteen people in rows. In Nepal such a capacity meant nothing. Passengers entered from the rear through full-width double doors. The lucky ones sat on wooden benches along each side. Later arrivals either squatted on the floor or sat on their baggage. Close quarters, unwashed peasants, and a chicken or two made for one interesting ride.

Frank was early and entitled to a bench seat. Waiting for the bus to fill, he took out the notice and read it over again a few more times. He tried to imagine what the hospital looked like. In his mind he saw Dr. Vigna as a very proper and compassionate man—a father figure eager to take young children in his arms. A mission hospital. Frank imagined a dedicated staff of kind nurses hovering devotedly over their patients like angels of mercy.

With a creaking jolt the bus left for Banepa. It swayed dangerously on the bends. The passengers would have been thrown around more inside but for the fact that they were jammed tight like cattle. Above them on the roof several dozen milk cans clattered about between metal rails.

Every few hundred yards, it seemed, there was a thump on the back door, and another person crowded in. Now and then, the driver climbed on top to unload the milk cans.

Gradually the bus climbed the low hills outside Kathmandu, winding its way up into still higher areas. They passed through small villages that looked unchanged from Bible times—each house an architectural feat of brick and timber, but with an ancient and worn appearance. The bus paused briefly at one village to allow a Hindu procession to work its way across. Dancers dressed in demonic outfits swirled ahead of the crowd.

"We need volunteer doctors . . ." The words sang in Frank's mind. They seemed to resonate with his underlying desire to be a useful part of God's creation.

At long last, the bus creaked into the cobbled square of a small village. Everyone got out of the bus. So this must be Banepa!

Frank walked down one of the main streets, stepping over the running sewage and animal waste. A few children playing in the middle of the road looked up as he passed and then returned to their game. A few shopkeepers peered disinterestedly from their alcoves as he walked by.

Someone had to know where the hospital was. He stopped an elderly Nepalese carrying a massive load of firewood on his back, supported by a band around his head. "Hospital-clinic?" he asked slowly. The man pointed down the street and continued on his way. Frank walked farther along the street. No hospital. Maybe the hospital didn't even exist.

"Hospital?" he asked a shopkeeper sitting among boxes of matches. The man pointed out of town.

Frank was beyond the town now. The road was narrowing fast to a single track. Maybe he was lost. He scanned the hillside ahead of him. Mostly farms, with a few huts. And on top of the hill—yes, it must be the hospital. His pace quickened as he strode toward it.

A young Nepalese woman hobbled toward him along the track from the building on top of the hill. She stopped as she passed, clasping both hands together and bowing in the traditional greeting, "Namaste." Her left foot was heavily bandaged, but she was smiling. "Doc-tor?" she asked.

"Yes. Doctor," answered Frank. It had been years since someone recognized him as a doctor. To most he was a hippie, a vagrant, a scruffy, untidy bum. And most times he took a special pleasure in being insulted that way.

"Hospital?" he asked, pointing to the low, tin-roofed building at the top of the rise. She nodded. This had to be it. He moved forward again in a fever pitch of anticipation.

Five years earlier his world turned and spun off its anchor. That day, he remembered, deep foreboding surged through his mind.

Now he had that same feeling—that his world was on the edge of another great change. There was a palpable pull from the hospital above. His empty self held back, but something else drew him on.

Go back to your cabin, said an ever-weakening voice inside. *Forget it all. You don't need it.*

This is where you belong, another part of him urged. *You will stay here; they need you here. You can help them.*

From the first moment he read the advertisement, Frank determined to offer himself to the hospital. He had already decided to stay. The temptation to board the plane and fly away was there, but he pushed it away.

Just before the hospital, the path climbs abruptly—so steeply that even a four-wheel drive vehicle will labor on the ascent. Frank barely noticed the grade. His heart was almost singing in anticipation. Something inside told him he was home.

In front of the hospital, he paused. Crowds of patients waited stoically outside the clinic. They turned to look at the American curiosity. "Dirty hippie," said one nurse to another in Hindi so that Frank couldn't understand. "I wonder what he wants here."

"I must see Dr. Vigna," said Frank, moving toward the nurses. "Where is Dr. Vigna?" They pointed him toward the front door. Someone took his arm and led him inside.

Dr. Vigna looked up from examining a patient. He was very much as Frank had imagined him. "Yes, can I help?" he said in a kindly way, his English accented by his Argentine origins.

"Dr. Vigna," said Frank, shaking his hand. "I read your notice." He held up the crumpled paper. "I am an American doctor. I've come to help at the hospital."

The director looked at him with a sympathetic gaze. Somehow he didn't seem bothered by Frank's unkempt appearance, his long hair, and rough beard.

"Are you prepared to stay here for at least two years?" he asked gently.

The memories raced in graphic fragments through Frank's mind—"Insubordinate," "dangerous," "we think you should leave."

"Yes," he said, "I will even sign a letter to guarantee it. I will stay two years."

Dr. Vigna squeezed his arm triumphantly. "Come with me," he said, leading Frank along the corridor to a small room with a concrete floor. "This is your office," he announced. "You are in charge of internal medicine."

"Thank you, Doctor." Frank shook the man's hand again.

"Come back tomorrow, and we will talk details," said Dr. Vigna with a smile. "In the meantime I must go back to my patients.

I can't believe this, Frank told himself. It was that simple. Just walk up and ask. He was committed to serve in a Third World mission hospital! God had been listening to him, that was obvious. This was not the result of blind chance.

He walked out into the sunshine of the hospital courtyard. *"Namaste."* A group of patients bowed in greeting. *"Namaste,* Doctor," said one.

Frank clasped his hands and bowed in reply. *"Namaste,"* he said, almost too overjoyed to speak.

I have to start looking like a doctor, he thought, with a start. *I must put on new clothes and have a shave.*

Frank paused a moment before he moved back down the hill to Banepa and the bus to Kathmandu. He looked at the modest little hospital and the crowds of patients. He could easily have shouted aloud. Never before had he been so thrilled after a climb.

16

NEW LIFE—
NEW FAMILY

F rank Kelly, mountain man and wanderer, never returned to Scheer Memorial. Early the next morning, a clean-shaven young American bounded up the hill in front of the hospital. Dr. Frank Kelly was reporting for long-term service to the Third World. Few people recognized him as the man of the day before.

There was plenty to do. Dr. Leonardo Vigna took the time to show Frank regular hospital procedures. At first, Frank stumbled in dealing with unfamiliar diseases. The old panic returned. *Maybe I have forgotten too much,* he thought. "Patience," encouraged Dr. Vigna. "It will soon come back to you." And it did.

Like a convalescing patient himself, Frank reveled in a growing sense of fulfillment. He found to his delight that the soul thrives on giving.

"*Namaste.*" He bowed to the stream of patients coming into the outpatient clinic. Soon Frank extended his vocabulary to more detailed conversation. The people laughed at his poor Nepali and patiently taught him a few more words. They reasoned that someone so anxious to speak their language must care for them.

The people's needs were basic. One day Frank noticed a commotion at the bottom of the hill below the hospital. "Someone must need help," he called to the nurse in the dispensary, as he picked up a medical kit and raced down the hill.

A crowd was gathered in a tight knot around something on the roadway. Frank pushed through the line of onlookers and almost drew back in horror. A young woman lay sprawled on the roadway, feebly attempting to rise and move on toward the hospital. A trail of red blood speckled the road behind her. The woman's dress was ripped and blood soaked. Her knees were deeply gashed from her desperate effort to crawl the remaining yards of cobbled roadway. It was obvious she needed help, but for some reason, a crowd of curious onlookers offered no assistance.

Aware of the watching crowd, Frank examined the woman as quickly and modestly as he could. He lifted her torn dress just enough to discover the problem. Even for a doctor, what he saw was distressing. The woman was giving birth to a child in the breech position. Her pain must have been unbearable.

How long she had suffered, Frank couldn't know. Clearly, the poor woman recognized that her only hope lay in reaching the hospital. She had traveled on foot from her village, the pain and damage increasing as she walked. A little farther, and she would have reached her goal. Dripping blood with each step, she dropped to a crawl and then collapsed in sight of her salvation.

Within a few minutes she lay on the operating table. The child was dead. A deft cut or two by the surgeon, and the body pulled free. They stitched the woman up, thinking her close to death. Several days later she walked back down that same path, going home to her village and telling everyone she met how wonderful the doctors were at Scheer Memorial. Simple, real needs and thankful patients: the best medicine for Dr. Kelly.

Almost immediately Frank discovered that Scheer Memorial was operated by the Seventh-day Adventist Church. More importantly, he realized that most of the staff were Adventist Christians. He couldn't help but notice. Each morning the staff met for a worship time together. Before every operation, Dr. Vigna bowed his head and prayed for skill and healing. At any moment of crisis there was prayer. And on Saturday they went to church. Frank went too.

At first he went because it was part of his big commitment. "I came here to work with these people," he rationalized. "Whatever their religion, whatever their ways, I am now part of it. I can't hold back."

He believed in God. Not the God of penance and purgatory—the God of his impressionable youth, the God he once accused of unfairness—a God who withheld love and life. Not even the God of the creeds and denominations he and Neal Isabelle discussed in army days. No, he believed in a God who created everything. A God of compassion. The God who created both the highest mountain and the lowest Nepalese.

Frank entered the small chapel that first Saturday Sabbath more curious than worshipful. True, no one pressured him to attend. They made no secret of the fact that Saturdays were sacred, but no one suggested he should worship with them. "Welcome, Frank." "Good to see you." "Come and sit with us." "We are always happy to see a new face, welcome!" Hardly high-pressure stuff. They didn't seem pushy, and they certainly were hospitable. He felt comfortable.

"Now, who can tell me the subject of our lesson this week?" Bible in hand, the teacher stood in front of his class and began to dialogue with them. The answer came quickly. Three people spoke at once, laughing at their shared eagerness. A few more leading questions from the teacher, and the entire class moved into an animated discussion of the Bible lesson.

At one point Frank volunteered his opinion on a text. The class members listened intently to his contribution. "Good point, Dr. Kelly," commented the teacher.

"I agree with Dr. Kelly," said an Indian nurse at the end of the pew. "Everytime I read that text . . ." her insight began another round of discussion.

Something stirred within Frank as he listened to these people talking openly and enthusiastically about spiritual concerns. This was nothing like the formal church ritual he was used to. Oh, yes, he once attended mass regularly and faithfully. But it was never interesting, never more than a boring duty.

Frank watched his new associates very closely. He listened carefully to every word they said, to every word the preacher of the day shared with the mission congregation. Of course, he was curious! More than curious, though; he needed to know if their religion was real. Were these people for real? He'd met too many religious hypocrites in the past; encountered too many denominations following foolish fables instead of the Bible.

That first Sabbath, Frank determined to learn more about Seventh-day Adventism. These people obviously enjoyed worshiping God. Their services were simple and interesting. Everything was open and nonjudgmental. It reminded him of the old-time religion, the pioneer, frontier religion of the United States. Maybe they had something.

"Have a happy Sabbath, Frank," said Dr. Vigna, shaking his hand after the church service. The doctor's grip was firm and reassuring.

"My husband is so pleased you've come to help us," said Mrs. Vigna. "There is so much to do."

"I'll stay as long as I'm needed," replied Frank.

"We are a small family here at the hospital," continued Mrs. Vigna. "You are part of it now."

Frank understood what she meant. Already he felt the closeness, the common bond. He said Goodbye to the Vignas and walked down the pathway toward the hospital. Off to one side the jagged Himalayan peaks sliced through the constant cloud cover. For the first time it struck him how strangely distant they appeared. Ahead of him were the hospital doors, opened wide to the afternoon breezes. Groups of patients sat on the veranda outside. "Namaste, Doctor," they chorused as he came closer.

He stopped for a few minutes to practice his Nepali on them. They laughed easily in the simple way of their country. One old lady was especially amused, slapping her thigh sharply in glee and smiling up at Frank in gap-toothed admiration. Too many foreigners never bothered to learn their language, but this doctor was different.

"You are a big hit, Dr. Kelly," said an Indian nurse standing nearby.

"They are such friendly people," Frank offered in a half-explanation. She nodded.

Frank heard some more distant laughter from a group of nurses and hospital workers coming down the road near the hospital. He watched them carefully. They seemed so happy.

Another peal of laughter, and he saw her. He had noticed the slight young nurse with the oriental features almost from the day he arrived.

"Who is that Chinese girl?" he asked the Indian nurse.

"That's Numami," she said, "but she is not Chinese. She is from Mizoram, a province of India near the Burmese border."

The group of nurses came closer. Numami was obviously the most outgoing among them. Her eyes sparkled with energy, and she moved with a quick grace.

"Hello, Numami," said Frank.

"It's the hippie American doctor," whispered one of the nurses in her ear. "The one with the long hair and beard."

"Hello, Frank Kelly," she answered well aware of his name. The beard and long hair were another thing. Numami had not seen Frank the first day he turned up to offer his services. To her he was the cleanshaven, almost shy doctor he appeared to be. Already the story of his wife's death had buzzed around the hospital and come to her ears. He needed help and friendship.

"Our group is going for a walk this afternoon," she said. "Would you like to come?" Of course he would. And so began his association with the singles' group at Scheer Memorial Hospital. Sometimes they went for walks together, sometimes they organized a games evening, and other times they had a special meal together.

Numami quickly assigned herself the task of helping Dr. Kelly. She knew he was lonely. So she went about lining up a lady friend for him.

"Frank," she said one day, stopping him in the hallway, "would you like to come and have a meal with me and a friend of mine?"

"Sure," he answered. "I'll look forward to it."

Numami's friend was an older volunteer nurse. *She's just perfect for Frank*, thought Numami, determined to arrange things.

The meal went very well. Frank obviously enjoyed himself. Karen seemed very interested in the young American doctor. It was hard to judge Frank's response, but he was very friendly with both of them, and they had a wonderful evening.

Numami engineered other get-togethers for Frank and Karen. There were no open signs that the two were attracted to each

other, but she persevered in her matchmaking. She had no way
of knowing that without her around, Frank and Karen had nothing to say. They shared long silences and awkward moments.

Frank and Numami spent hours discussing religion. "Why do
you keep Saturday as a worship day?" he asked her early on in
their dialogues.

"Because the Bible says we must," Numami answered prompt-
ly. "The fourth commandment is very clear. Let me show you."
She picked up a Bible and showed him the words in Exodus.
"The Bible is God's Word for us," she said. "We must obey what
God says." Frank agreed with her.

"Thou shalt not kill," he read, determined to follow it with a
trick question. "I was a soldier once. Soldiers have to kill. What
do you say to that?"

"Adventists don't believe in killing," she maintained. "Our
young men refuse to carry weapons. They are conscientious ob-
jectors. If they are drafted into the army, they request work as
medics—healing people, not killing."

Frank liked that. It agreed with his pacifist ideas. "Adventists
are different in many ways, aren't they?" he commented.

"We don't smoke, we don't drink . . ." began Numami.

"I like that," said Frank. "I think those habits are disgusting.
People who deal in alcohol and tobacco are exploiting the lives of
others for their personal gain." He had strong ideas about the
corruption of society.

"In many ways I'm already an Adventist," he told Numami
one day.

"There's a lot more," she replied. "You should study all the different Bible doctrines we believe."

"I will," he answered. "The day I arrived here I decided to
learn more about worshiping God."

The daily hospital routine itself was changing Frank. Each
patient, each ulcer he swabbed, each child he held, drew him
closer to a knowledge of a caring God. After hours, the patients
knocked on his door. "Doctor, help us please," they begged. No
longer did he imagine himself an empty husk that roamed aimlessly—he was needed, he was fulfilling a God-given duty.

"Inasmuch as ye have done it unto one of the least of these . . .
ye have done it unto me," read the preacher one Sabbath. His

patients were God's special charge. What a privilege to help them. "Come quickly, Frank," a nurse tugged at his sleeve. "Numami is very ill. She can't get out of bed."

Frank dropped his papers on the desk and raced out the door after her. "What is the matter?" he gasped at a run.

"I think she passed a stone. She seems to be in terrible pain. She needs help." The nurse led him quickly up the road to Numami's little apartment.

Frank's mind was in a whirl of anxiety. Numami was such a nice young woman. Already she was a close friend—after just a few days. *Please, God, don't let her get sick.*

Numami lay very still under the sheets. Frank pulled back the sheet gently and touched her abdomen. She leaped to her feet in an instant. "April fools!" she laughed. The other nurses behind the door in the next room leaped out in great glee at the prank.

A great joke. After the first flush of embarrassment, Frank laughed too. But there was something else. He realized that already Numami was a special part of his life. He said nothing to her of his new feelings.

Two other doctors joined the staff within weeks of Frank's arrival. Devanan David, a young Indian resident, came shortly after. With his help the workload eased a little, although the constant stream of patients would have taxed a dozen doctors.

Then in early May Dr. Nestor Hein and his family arrived from Argentina. Nestor was a classmate of Leonardo Vigna and his designated replacement as medical director. From the beginning, he and Frank got along famously.

"Nestor, would you be willing to study Adventist beliefs with me?" Frank asked.

"Of course," answered his new friend. "So long as you understand it'll take more than an hour or two."

"I want to learn all about the church," said Frank. He hardly guessed the lessons would take twenty-four weeks.

After the April fools joke, things moved quickly with Numami. Frank was very shy about any open statement of affection. Just the same they both knew something was happening. Numami gave up on her efforts to pair Frank off with Karen. It was obvious the chemistry wasn't there.

"I'm going to join the Adventist Church," Frank told Numami

one evening in mid-May. "Nestor has already taken me through the basics, and I believe it all. I'm ready to dedicate my life to Christ and serve Him here."

"That's wonderful, Frank." Numami beamed. Whatever her affection for him, all along, her primary goal had been his commitment to God. She wanted Frank to know God and the happiness that comes from Him.

They both stood in the gentle Himalayan moonlight looking out through the trees to the lights of Banepa below the hill. Frank turned to Numami, hesitating a little before he spoke.

"Numami," he said, "I'm not much of a catch. But would you be willing to marry this old man?"

She looked at him with accepting eyes. "I love you, Frank," she answered quietly. "If you will be happy married to a young Mizo girl, I will marry you."

Frank embraced Numami tenderly. "You are the world to me," he assured.

"And Snesia?" she asked, fearful of a rival she had never known.

"Snesia is dead," said Frank calmly. "This is my new home, and you are the woman I love. There is a wonderful future ahead of us."

They announced their engagement to the hospital staff on May 16. Of course, there were happy congratulations. Frank and Numami were so obviously in love, although before their announcement, few guessed at anything more than friendship.

"Be careful," warned one of Numami's friends a little later. "He's a wanderer. He'll walk off and leave you. He'll go back to America and leave you here."

Numami said nothing. Frank was not like that, she knew. There was only one condition to her marriage with Frank. He said he intended to join the church. She believed him. When that happened, they would marry.

"I want to be baptized when the studies are over," Frank told Nestor. "I intend to join the Seventh-day Adventist Church and work here at the hospital as long as the church wants me to."

How long Frank stayed in Nepal depended more on the laws of the state than any church decision. His working permit was about to expire.

"We've had no success in applying for your work permit," Nestor told him at last. "This government is very suspicious of foreigners wanting to live here."

"What can I do?" asked Frank. "I don't want to leave."

"There's only one thing you can do," Nestor answered. "Buy a bus ticket to India. Renew your tourist visa for Nepal, and then come back. That will give you six more months."

It was an awkward plan, but the only way.

On occasions church leaders from around the world visited the hospital to offer encouragement and gather firsthand information from the field. Dr. Gordon Hadley, director of the medical department at church headquarters in Washington, D.C., USA, stopped by on a tour of India and the Far East. In the course of visiting with the staff, he met Frank and heard his story.

"No work permit," he said. "We must do what we can at once. It's obvious that the Lord wants you here, Frank."

"So far the government has turned down all requests for a permit," explained Nestor.

"We musn't give up," said Dr. Hadley. "Who do we know in Kathmandu that can help?"

"Paul Dalhunty, our ADRA (Adventist Development and Relief Association) representative there may know someone," suggested Nestor.

"Well, let's get hold of him right away," urged Dr. Hadley. "We've no time to lose." He turned back to Frank. "I understand you are requesting baptism?"

"That's right, sir," said Frank. "Just as soon as Nestor completes the Bible-study course with me."

Nestor nodded his approval. "Frank understands Adventist beliefs very well," he assured Dr. Hadley. "He is carrying regular responsibilities here. After his baptism he should be formally posted here as a missionary doctor."

"Is this what you want, Frank?" asked Dr. Hadley.

"It is the greatest desire of my life," answered Frank. "The day I came to the hospital I dedicated my life to serve these people. What I have learned about Adventism has only increased my commitment."

"Then we must process a call for you," said the church leader, using a biblical term the church uses for a formal request to overseas service. "When does your return ticket expire?" he asked suddenly, struck by an idea.

"Early January," said Frank, not sure of the exact date.

"Let's do this. Use your ticket and return to the States by year-end. With no regular pastor at the hospital, it's awkward to arrange a baptism here. So you can be baptized in America, we will process your appointment to begin January 1, and . . . and that will be it," concluded Dr. Hadley in his usual energetic fashion.

It all sounded so easy. A dream come true. But for now, there was the trouble with the work permit. *One step at a time; don't rush it,* thought Frank.

Dr. Hadley left a few days later. "I'll see you in California," he promised. "Everything will work out, you'll see." Frank's visa deadline came up and no work permit had come.

"What can be so bad about a bus trip to India, anyway?" he wondered aloud as he set off. Numami embraced him at the roadside as the battered bus came in sight. "God bless you, Frank," she wished. "Come back soon." Only a few days away, and yet the ache he felt inside told him he could never permanently leave this new love.

The bus bounced slowly to Kathmandu. Perched on the engine hump inside, close against several dozen curious villagers, Frank knew the trip to India would be a trial. At the depot in Kathmandu he searched around for the bus to India. Not in yet. There was just time to drop by and see Paul Dalhunty. At least Paul had tried to arrange the permit.

"Frank!" Paul met him at the door. "You'll never believe what just happened." The normally calm Australian was just bubbling with excitement. "I called a friend of mine yesterday asking for his help with your permit. He just now phoned me to say he contacted a government minister friend of his . . . and the minister said come right over."

"What are we waiting for!" Frank beamed. "Let's take a taxi and get over there right now."

The minister listened intently to Frank's story when they arrived at his office. It was clear he already knew the details. "I think we can arrange your work permit," he said kindly. "Our people have a great need for medical help."

"Five years!" exulted Frank later. "The permit is good for five years." Five years was a long time. So much had happened in the previous five years. So much he needed to forget—memories of Snesia, aimless wandering in search of fulfillment, halfhearted attempts at love and work. The next five years were sure to be special. God was in charge now.

The end of the year came quickly. Twenty-four weeks of Bible studies went by in an exciting blur of affirmation. Yes, Frank was ready for baptism. He couldn't wait to make his public declaration of love to a God who had tracked him so patiently over the years.

"Come back soon, Frank" said Numami whenever they discussed the trip to America. "I know you'll come back soon."

"Sure I will, honey," he told her, holding her close each time. He knew a few cynics still warned her that he would fly away for good one day. They didn't really know him. They didn't really know the man who was willing to sacrifice all for love.

"I want the best for you, Numami," he told her. "Even if we do have to delay the wedding a bit." She didn't like the idea of any delay beyond January.

"You should take those extra nursing courses you told me about," he said. "It's necessary for your career."

"But that will mean eighteen months in India—away from you." She protested. "Eighteen months from next June!"

"I'll wait here," promised Frank. Numami looked into his eyes and knew it was the truth.

They kissed goodbye at the airport in Kathmandu. Numami waved happily to Frank as he moved through customs. He would come back a baptized, commissioned missionary doctor. Soon he would be her husband. It was all in God's hands.

The Royal Nepal Airlines jet rushed down the runway and up across the wide Kathmandu Valley. Frank looked down as it dropped away beneath him. It looked like home! He traced the narrow road up into the hills at Banepa. Already the plane was too high for him to make out the hospital itself. Just the same, he saw it all clearly in his mind's eye. He saw it there above the sharply rising track. He saw the needy patients, grateful and friendly, waiting at the clinic door for his return. And a Mizo nurse still praying for him.

A few days later, on January 2, 1988, Frank Kelly died. Frank Kelly, rebel, the man who shunned society, the inconsolable widower, was left behind forever in the watery grave of baptism. More than a symbol, the ceremony marked the public commitment of the new Frank Kelly, Seventh-day Adventist missionary doctor to Nepal.

The thousands of people in the Loma Linda University Church listened sympathetically as Frank briefly outlined the events in his life leading up to his decision to join the church.

Then Pastor Louis Venden led Frank into the waters of the baptismal font. He turned and addressed the crowd before the ceremony. "Frank Kelly has come a long way to make his public commitment today," he said. "You have heard his story. Normally we ask that family members stand as a relative is baptized. Frank has no family here today. But I invite all who will to stand as his brothers and sisters in Christ."

Pastor Venden placed one arm around Frank's shoulders and raised the other high above him. "Frank Kelly," he said in a loud, joyous voice, "today you've come here with the desire to make a public statement of your commitment to the Lord Jesus Christ. It's my privilege to baptize you in the name of the Father, the Son, and the Holy Spirit." The entire congregation stood to its feet as the pastor lowered Frank in the water.

Welcome to the family, Frank.

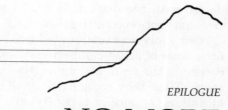

NO MORE
MOUNTAINS

T he cassette tape wound down to its hub, and the recorder switched off with a sharp snap. I reached for another tape.

"We've been talking for quite a while," said Frank, rising from his wicker chair and stretching his arms wide. "How about we take a break! Let's walk back to the hospital and see what's going on."

He'd told his story willingly and given freely of his time, but I knew how the hospital drew him. His life is now inextricably tied up with the people of Nepal and their needs.

My wife came toward us across the open patio of the Horizon Hotel. "We've finished for the day, Rosa Delia," announced Frank, sure that she, too, wanted a break. "I was just telling Lincoln that we should walk down to the hospital. Numami will be off duty by the time we get there too."

The three of us turned down the trail along the ridge to Banepa and the hospital. It was only a mile away, around several folds in the valley.

"It's beautiful, isn't it?" remarked Frank, waving his hand in a wide sweep across the vista of terraced gardens and small farmhouses perched on narrow outcrops. Many of the fields were

177

dotted with the distant figures of women bending low over the rice and root-crop cultivation.

Our reply was interrupted by the chatter of children. A tight little knot of schoolchildren just out of class charged around the corner in the trail. Seeing us, they stopped speechless for a moment. Then they recognized Dr. Kelly and crowded round him, all talking at once in eager Nepali.

We walked on with the children swirling around us. A few of the bolder boys showed off by leaping over the steep dropaway next to the high path. A rock pushed over the edge would roll unchecked for several thousand feet. The sure-footed boys shrieked with laughter at our concern.

"That's my sister," said one little fellow of about six. "Take her picture," he pleaded, tugging at the camera in my hand and pointing down below the trail. Several young women working on a lower terraced field looked up at us. "There she is," said the boy in quite good English. "Take her picture." I obliged, and he seemed satisfied. The act of taking the picture was enough for him; he hardly cared about the photograph itself.

"They are so friendly," my wife remarked as the children laughed and giggled along the way. She ran on ahead with some of them in an impromptu race. They kept pace with her easily, their bare little feet slapping the ground as they ran.

Frank watched them pensively. "It's a hard life here," he said. The thought seemed to remind him of our earlier conversation. "After my baptism I stayed on in the United States for another two months." Quite a statement from the man who at that time was clearly in love with Nepal and Numami. I would have expected him to rush back after the baptism and his formal posting to the hospital.

"I traveled around the U.S. for two months," he repeated, "visiting my old friends. It was odd—when I met my old friends, my old climbing buddies. We hugged each other, and I was happy to see them. But something had changed. They seemed a part of another life.

"Everywhere I went I met with Seventh-day Adventists. I even met Dr. Stanley Sturges, the doctor who established Scheer Memorial Hospital back in 1957. I spoke to congregations in Dallas, Texas; Rochester, New York; Boston, Massachusetts; and

Portland, Oregon—many places. Everywhere, it was the same. Warm, welcoming people—friends at once; almost like family members. One of my greatest regrets is that I didn't get to know Adventists sooner."

The road ahead of us dipped slightly, opening up the view toward Banepa. On top of a nearby hill stood Scheer Memorial Hospital. Even at a distance I could see the steady stream of patients moving up and down the road from town.

"That was the bonus part of my two months . . ." Frank obviously stayed for another reason. "At the request of the Adventist Development and Relief Agency, I spent most of that time visiting at different medical institutions, telling them of the needs in Nepal. Of course, I went to Huntington, West Virginia, where I contacted many of the doctors I once worked with."

Frank looked across the valley toward the hospital, then turned to Rosa and me. "There are so many generous people. I was promised dozens of near-new hospital beds, hundreds of thousands of dollars worth of equipment, and many cash donations."

A few minutes later we turned through Banepa and up the little mountain trail leading to the hospital. Frank clasped his hands and dipped them to the smiling patients we passed on our way up. "*Namaste,* Doctor," they murmured politely.

At the top of the hill we paused while Frank chatted in Nepali to a group of patients sitting cross-legged on the grass. The three women talked in the low, respectful tone of the hill people. Their conversation was easy and relaxed. It was obvious they valued the attentions of a doctor who cared enough to ask about their concerns in their own language. Nothing could ever erase the cultural differences, yet beyond language, Frank's jauntily worn Nepalese cap emphasized communication.

The hospital was in a mess the day we arrived. I'll not hide the news of their disarray. Frank was even proud of it.

"We are building a whole new wing to the hospital, as well as extra staff apartments," he said as a workman trundled past with a wheelbarrow load of handmade bricks. "The two-story brick addition will give us more than double our present capacity, plus new offices for staff and a new clinic." The clinic meant a lot to Frank.

The half-finished addition rose high behind a bamboo grid of scaffolding and mounds of tumbled brick. It was an inspiring sight. Tomorrow in process. A bright future.

"Do patients pay enough to support this expansion?" I questioned, knowing the answer too well. Bare feet and tattered clothing around us signaled a No to the question.

Frank shook his head. "This is only possible because of generous believers around the world," he said. "Without their help the hospital could not operate."

"Doctor, come quickly. There is an emergency." A nurse tugged at Frank's arm and darted back into the dark hallway of the old hospital. Frank ran to keep up with her, grabbing his medical kit at the nurse station.

A small girl of perhaps five lay on a simple cot in the hallway. Her eyes were rolled back. She gasped for breath with an effort that arched her entire body. The air rattled in her throat.

"Pneumonia," said Frank, listening to the child's lungs through his stethoscope. "I'm afraid it's advanced too far for us to help her much." He spoke gently to the worried mother in low Nepali. "Tell me if there is any change," he said in English to the Indian nurse.

"*Namaste,* Doctor," the mother said with sad, trusting eyes as we left.

"Come and see our apartment," suggested Frank, needing to change the subject. We moved away from the main hospital toward an even older building off to one side. "It's a little cramped, but it's home," said Frank, obviously wanting us to be prepared for the worst.

At our approach an old woman and three children jumped up from the concrete landing behind the apartment. They were extremely dirty and disheveled. "*Namaste,*" said the woman in a high-pitched voice, showing her almost toothless gums. The children ran toward Frank, calling out something in their own language.

"What are they saying?" asked my wife.

Frank laughed a little self-consciously. "They are calling me Daddy! This lady, not nearly as old as she looks, by the way— probably in her mid-twenties—is a widow. She and her children became beggars when the father died. They turned up on our doorstep some months ago. We fed them, and they've lived on our landing ever since. They obviously think that by calling me Daddy they put me under obligation."

He knocked on the door. Numami answered it at once. Her expressive face broke into a smile immediately. "Hello, dear," she said. "I've been expecting you for a while."

Frank embraced her and beckoned us through the door. We sat down at the table as Frank poured us all a cool fruit drink. Numami left for a moment and returned with a photo album. "Our wedding pictures," she said proudly.

"When was the wedding?" my wife asked with that special interest that women always give to the subject.

"April 27, this year—1988," answered Numami, the date still a fresh, exciting memory.

"Why, you are just newlyweds," I exclaimed. "That's less than five months ago."

"We had planned to wait a while longer, but . . . well, a lot of things happened to change our minds. I think it was all for the best to move the date up. We're happy together," concluded Frank, squeezing Numami's hand.

"Look at this picture," she said, opening the album to a photograph of the entire wedding party, guests and all. "It was a special wedding," she remembered happily.

"We put up a big tent in front of the hospital," said Frank, "and invited everybody. We wanted our Nepalese friends to enjoy the day with us."

"Everybody came," added Numami. "See that man." She pointed to a man in the photo. "He is Sailendra Kumar Upadya, the foreign minister. And there—the mayor of Dhulikhel, a little town near here. Oh, and my mother came . . ." She was about to continue when she heard a baby cry in the next room. In a moment Numami was up and back with a very young baby in her arms.

"This is Mickey Maya," she announced.

"Mickey's mother is an emotionally disturbed peasant girl," explained Frank. "They found her and the newborn baby out in the fields, covered with cow dung. We are caring for Mickey until we can find a home for her."

Rosa Delia pulled back the cloth around the baby's face. "She's such a beautiful baby," she said.

"We think so," replied Numami. "It will be hard to give her up. Still, Frank and I will have one of our own one day soon."

Without needing to play back the cassette, I remembered Frank's regrets after Snesia's death. No child to remind him of her. The woman who shared so many of his interests—gone. I knew that he would never totally forget the past.

But just as surely, I knew that he had found a future. Numami and he share a special love, a common faith, and the rewards of service to others.

Outside once more, the four of us walked down the road toward the hospital. In the low light of a setting sun the hospital had a warm red glow. Beyond it, dressed in colder gray, the high peaks of the Himalayas.

I needed the answer to one last question.

"Do you ever go climbing in those mountains?"

Frank looked at Numami as he held her close in the sudden chill of the evening. "Never," she said. "Never."

* * * * *

Publisher's note—

As this book goes to press, Frank and Numami are back in the United States. Frank's father was suddenly taken ill, and they returned to be with the family. Frank's father recovered and is doing well.

In a few days, Numami is due to give birth to their first child.

They have so much to be thankful for. However, the dark cloud resting over their happiness has come in the form of news from Nepal that Frank's work permit may be rescinded by the government. Whatever the outcome and wherever God may lead them, Frank and Numami remain committed to a life of service.

Snesia—
the "snow maiden."

Frank and Snesia with her
parents, Milan and Radmila
Zdravkovich, in 1975.

Frank with his brother's children in
Chicago (chapter 12). One of the
low points in Frank's life after
Snesia's death.

Frank and Snesia share a relaxed
moment with Frank's sister Kat.

Frank as he appeared in February 1987 during the trip to Nepal.

A passenger bus similar to the one Frank rode to Banepa when he first went to Scheer Memorial. No padded seats here—just two wooden planks along each side.

Scheer Memorial Hospital. Construction of new wing is well under way.

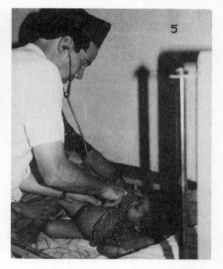

A reborn Frank Kelly discovers a new purpose in life as a doctor to the Nepalese people.

Numami—
a new love and a new life.

April 27, 1988—a new beginning.

Dr. Frank Kelly and Numami with visiting German medical student who discovered hospital while trekking and stayed on for six months of volunteer service. The trio is standing on the main street of Dhulikel, near the hospital.

A back view of the new residents' quarters. In left foreground is the concrete landing behind the Kelly apartment, where a displaced Nepalese family live.

Dr. Kelly with his patients in the "waiting room."

Surrounded by admirers, Frank makes his way up a track leading to the hospital.

On a Sabbath afternoon hike in the hills near the hospital, Frank pauses for a moment with his guide for the day, Chanerakancha, a maintenance worker at Scheer.